HELP!
I Run a Sunday School

BOOKS BY MARY DUCKERT
PUBLISHED BY THE WESTMINSTER PRESS

Help! I Run a Sunday School
Help! I'm a Sunday School Teacher

HELP!
I Run a Sunday School

by Mary Duckert
Illustrated by Donald W. Patterson

W
The Westminster Press
Philadelphia

ISBN 0-664-24930-2
Library of Congress Catalog Card No. 77-158124

PUBLISHED BY THE WESTMINSTER PRESS ®
PHILADELPHIA, PENNSYLVANIA

PRINTED IN THE UNITED STATES OF AMERICA

In memory of Hulda Niebuhr
Florence Stubbs
and
Ruth Gibbons Graves
who never gave up on the church school

contents

preface

In recent years it has become a popular parlor game among some professional churchmen to run down the church school enterprise. Some of those people have found workable substitutes for it; some have ignored it even to its death; some have stepped in to work alongside the volunteers in an effort to make the whole thing worthwhile.

Of this I am sure: church schools will seldom be more than a waste of time if teachers and leaders do not approach their jobs with a joyous urgency. If we have no story to tell, no heritage to pass on to the young, and no attitudes toward life to communicate, we are participants in an unholy fraud.

I am also sure of one more thing: parlor games are not likely to affect the existence of the church school when even a small remnant in a congregation is determined to work together for a sound educational system. What we all need is encouragement, education, good resources, and the esteem of those around us.

When I wrote *Help! I'm a Sunday School Teacher* it was my sturdy conviction that without those men and women who teach, there would be no school. I still believe that. As a director of Christian education—sometimes to the fury of my fellow educators—I regard myself as the *servant* not *center* of the educational work in the church.

Coordinators, superintendents, lead teachers, committee chairmen, directors, ministers, and assistants in Christian education—whatever our jobs—are expected to work with the sole purpose of improving the teachers' lot in our churches. It is the intention of this book to encourage you in that work, share with you what others have done, and assure you that the teachers are in immediate need of the support you can give them.

M.D.

introduction:
you and
your job

Being a responsible organization man in Operation Church School for the first time is like finding yourself in charge of a major-league baseball team. After you assess what you have going for and against you as a manager, you look at the team you were given, you give some concrete thought to the players and coaches you've yet to get, you set some modest objectives concerning performance, and then you look at yourself and the whole operation again long and hard. Only then are you ready to start working for the club.

The secret of the effective, well-run church school—and we'll give you that right away—is that three fifths of the work has been done before the teachers and pupils come together. The teachers have prepared, the administration has planned, organized, and distributed supplies and curriculum materials. And they have found a place for every teacher and pupil who come. Last and most important, the teachers and administrators have planned and studied together for their mutual good and the welfare of the learners.

The two fifths of the work we can see are the performance in the classroom and the active support of people like you, whose job it is to observe, assess, and *help* the teachers do a good job.

You'll soon find, if you don't already know it, that you can't do the job by yourself, no matter how small an operation your church school is. Keeping an adequate school in good running order takes more than one body with one mind and only one pair of legs.

In a very small church in California, a young couple attending the congregational service of worship for the first time were audibly startled to hear the pastor read a letter of directions from his *wife* to various members of the congregation. A friendly soul in front of them turned around and whispered, "She's president of the Women of the Church, superintendent of the church school, teacher of the midweek Bible class, and poor thing broke her hip ringing the bell last week."

"Poor thing," the visiting man mumbled, "probably needed a good long rest anyway."

No ball club is at its best if one person tries to be manager, coach, and player. You need to spread the work around and in so doing, *organization* is born. And just as man is not made for the Sabbath, but the Sabbath for man, so organization is intended to make life simpler rather than to complicate, confound, and confuse. The structure of your school may resemble many others, but if that structure serves you well, it is probably unlike any other anywhere.

WHERE TO BEGIN

We all begin with ourselves. What am I to do? Where do I belong in the order of events? Why was I asked to do anything at all?

WHAT AM I TO DO?

Often—too often—and this may be your situation, no clear picture of administrative responsibilities is drawn. As successor you are expected to do what your predecessor did, and if he's moved out of town, you're either in or out of luck. You can make your own job based on observation, reading, and horse sense.

If you're the minister. Several years ago an interim minister at a Presbyterian church in the Midwest gathered the six nonteaching persons on the church school staff for an "orientation," he called it. (One of the six had been a departmental superintendent for twenty-six years.) He preceded his lecture, as it turned out to be, with the comment that since he was temporary and pensioned, he could at last do and say what he'd never had courage enough to say before.

What he said was that the day had long since gone by when administrators did not have to know about techniques and content of teaching. Then he drew a diagram resembling an ice cream cone. He said, in explanation: "I am at the tip of the cone as moderator of the session. The session is above me as decision maker for the church. The Christian education committee is next, supported by me and the session. You are above us, working in our place. The teachers are on the top of the cone supported by all of us. You can expect help from those underneath on the cone. Likewise, you exist in the church school to help those above you."

At the end of the lecture, the veteran of twenty-six years

said, "You taught me something tonight, but I'm not going to tell you what it is."

"I turned the cone upside down, didn't I, Helen?" he responded.

"Why did it take me twenty-six years to see it that way? It's so simple and sensible," she confessed.

"Why did I wait until I was sixty-eight years old to give teachers the support I knew they needed?" He smiled, and the conversation was over.

Whatever the details of your job, the intention is to *support* the leaders and teachers—to help them be adequate in their jobs. Start there with *what* you are to do.

If you're on the church school committee. Committees in charge of the church school are of two kinds: (1) working or (2) advisory. To say that one committee is advisory does not, of course, mean that the members are idle. It simply means that committee participation does not involve working regularly with an age group or in another responsible post in the church school. The advisory committee very often is made up of people who have worked in the church school, those involved in secular education, a member or two from the official board, the minister, and the superintendent, who does not vote.

A working committee may be made up of departmental superintendents, with the superintendent as chairman.

Generally, when the committee is advisory, its duties and scope go beyond the church school, including adult study groups, choirs, summer activities, and community youth involvement. It acts for the official board of the church and is sometimes appointed by them. If you are on such a committee, you have probably shown an interest or knowledge of a particular subject area or age group. It is your job, then, to become acquainted with those persons working in that area in your church's educational program. What materials and supplies do they work with? Under what conditions do they lead and teach? What difficulties or obstacles confront them? What further educational opportunities might help them? Part of being an adviser is learning to listen, observe, and work out solutions in concert with those who have the problems.

Working committees know what the problems are. They're very close to them. If you work both in the church school and as a decision maker for the church school, you face the danger of being too close to the situation to recognize the extent of the educational problems. When you're busy with details of schedules, supplies, curriculum orders, absent teachers, and new enrollees, it is sometimes hard to remember that even more important than all these things is treating *people* in the church school as the neighbors they are. Listening and talking over difficulties are of utmost importance to the well-being of the whole school. As a favor to yourself and every child and teacher there, take time to be of help when it is most needed.

A fairly new church on the West Coast began with a working education committee of five departmental superintendents and the general superintendent. They made great educational strides in the first three years of the church's existence. Within five years, however, they were barely able to function. The school had tripled in size during its fourth and fifth years, building plans were under way, and school was held in the church sanctuary, the small educational unit, and a lodge hall several blocks away.

The superintendent spoke with the governing board of the church. He pleaded for extra hands and extra minds to solve insurmountable problems, as he called them. An advisory group, representative of the total church education enterprise, was appointed. As a result of working with the former committee, many informed decisions were made. The new committee had the advantage of experienced workers familiar with the teachers, children, and operation of the school, and the objective, inquiring stance of those most recently appointed.

Makeup of a committee is not a once-and-for-all decision. A committee exists to serve a need. As soon as needs change so should the functions and makeup of committees. Your job as a committee is to clear the way for sound education in your church. Your job as a committee member is to find out what your specific assignment is to be, and to do it without delay.

If you're the church school superintendent or coordinator. Though the expectations of churches vary when it comes to the performance in jobs with these names, your main responsibility is organizational. As one diminutive, twenty-three-year-old new broom was told: "There's nothing much to it. Just see that everything runs well." She did. She calculated that it took her three eight-hour days a week, Sunday mornings, and about three evening meetings a month. She was an organizer only. Education was the province of the minister of education and the senior pastor. When asked at an educational event to list a few of her duties for one year, she wrote quickly:

> make class lists
> help Ted get new teachers
> get material to teachers
> call new teachers together
> gather departments for big meeting
> meet with Christian education committee
> order materials for study
> order supplies and keep track of them
> watch budget
> record attendance weekly
> coordinate all-school projects
> make room assignments
> ask teachers to teach another year
> get substitutes

She was not finished when it came time for her to report. A minister of education in the group, with growing irritation, finally asked, "What do your ministers do?"

They did a great deal, she felt, in the areas of teaching Biblical content, teaching techniques, and pastoral counseling. No one was competent to observe in the classrooms, however, and it was for that reason she was taking advantage of this educational event.

It's possible that because you are willing to take on a big job like the one this woman had, your church officers are willing to make it even bigger. There's no rule except the one of diminishing returns in operation here. If you're trying to take the jobs of six people instead of helping thirty people do their work well, you might find that in spite of your remarkable versatility and unbounded energy, your well-organized church school staff is not doing an adequate job of *teaching*. You and the people who appointed you should find out from one another what the expectations are for the school and the job. Someone needs to organize the operation. Volunteers need education, orientation, and support. At some time or other every teacher needs help in his classroom. Think deep and long before you decide you can serve well in all these areas simultaneously.

If you're being paid for whatever you're doing. Some few churches traditionally pay departmental and general superintendents. The thinking is that from those who are given a little, much can be required. *Required* is the important word; they are no longer volunteers who can say "no" or "maybe." Over the years, this plan of "a lot for a little" has not worked so effectively as a few of its originators believed it would. The semiprofessional perennial admits that it is not money but satisfaction that keeps him coming. Being a part-time popcorn salesman, window washer, dog walker, or telephone solicitor all pay more.

Many churches hire what they call "assistants in Christian education." These people act as directors of Christian education for less money and often with less formal education. Sometimes they are even more able than D.C.E.'s in the areas in which the professional is expected to excel. Though it cannot be said that they are a lot better or more valuable than professionals, by their sheer number they are certainly as useful to the church.

If you are employed to assist in Christian education, you have a right as a fellow Christian and/or church member to discuss and determine with your governing board just what is expected of you in approximately how many hours and for how much money.

A good many of us don't mind admitting we're overworked or underappreciated, but we somehow believe we're being foes of Christ if we mention money. If you really are overworked, it's likely that someone appreciated you very much, and he well may be one who could be sharing your work load. You're not giving your work away when you delegate responsibility. Delegating is part of your work. It builds strong, capable leaders for the days when you are no longer there.

If you don't know how much money is fair to expect, ask area Christian education consultants or headquarters personnel people from your denomination or another if yours has no help available. Of one thing you can be sure, you will never be overpaid if you do your job. And if you don't, no amount is too small.

WHERE DO I BELONG?

This question doesn't mean where do you stand during church school, but that's part of it. You can't decide even that until you and your associates get together and determine what duties belong to whom. Sometimes they're a surprise to everyone.

A church school superintendent with one year's experience began his second year thinking he served no useful purpose. The school was closely graded with an effective lead teacher at every grade level and what were called coordinators for children under first grade, grades one through six, youth, and adults. There was also a director of Christian education. The superintendent's co-workers pleaded with him to stay, and he did, reluctantly. The second Sunday morning after the school reopened in the fall, he was languishing in the downstairs corridor when a teacher fell to the floor and a child of eight came for him. He ran to get a doctor who was teaching fourth grade, called for an ambulance, and most likely, said the doctor in charge of the woman's heart, saved her life.

At his retirement seven years later an elder gave him a touching and amusing tribute. He said that during that second crucial year, he washed off skinned knees, placated and carried two-year-olds who were lonesome for their parents, persuaded an avid football fan on his way to the game that he should *wait* until the fifth grade dismissed before squiring his daughter from the church, and thawed out a pair of ears white with a northeast winter.

During the time he was there, the teachers knew there was a minuteman they could count on. The elder who gave the tribute said he was their "insurance policy" for every eventuality. He was neither soldier nor document. He was a man who was available when things happened. A fellow you could count on to be there.

The year he left, a new minister came, the director of Christian education left, the school became departmentalized, and the new superintendent reigned over a course called "Help for New Teachers." He was definitely a different kind of superintendent from his predecessor. But, if the school was doing its job, *someone* was teaching teachers and someone else was "floating" in the corridors.

There is no "spozed to be" for church school organization. The job of organizing is harder than in business, because there are no rules to lean upon. Each church makes its own rules as new people take new jobs.

BUT WHY ME?

Personnel committees and individuals faced with filling vacancies in the church school aren't consistent in their search for a first-rate staff. You can assume they knew quality when they saw you, if you want to. It's likely, though, that they saw someone without quite enough to do and found you willing.

The important word is *willing*. That's where good leadership begins. If you are willing to learn, work, and evaluate your efforts, you're well on your way toward a job worth doing.

Teaching a class of children, young people, or adults for the first time is no song, but there are built-in securities such as materials to work with and an established curriculum. Supervising and administrating have those things secondarily. The primary concern is adults doing what they were asked to do.

At an annual meeting of Christian educators a woman and man were playing the verbal game "I do too work harder than you do." The man worked eighty hours a week. The woman didn't *know* how many hours she worked. The man had sent three quarters of his staff to summer school for a week. The woman had had a very well attended leadership education series in the fall. A new director of Christian education with less than a year's experience was noticeably awed by the feats of the two. "Maybe you can tell me how best to use my time during the church school sessions. I can't be everywhere at once," she said.

The man assisted in the services of worship running concurrently with the church school sessions and seldom witnessed what went on. The woman told the newcomer to her profession: "Don't bother to go into the classrooms. They don't want you anyway."

"Well, how can you help them if you don't know what they need?" the younger and possibly wiser woman asked.

Your job, before any other responsibility, is to support those people with whom you work. You are to be dependable.

A woman who had been lead teacher for a generation of five-year-olds broke her back and was in a walking cast for a long time. The other teachers took turns leading while she watched and finally took over completely. After the first week of her absence, she received a note from one of the teachers: "It wasn't the work you did, Ruth. We can do that. It was your support. You were so *there,* and last Sunday you weren't."

So be there. What you do from then on is what this whole book is about.

the veterans on your team

From the outside, the number one problem in the church school is: How do you get new teachers? From the inside, to a new administrator, the problem is: How do you get along with the old ones?

They aren't demons, and even those with a reputation for being impeccable want very much to live in unity. They show it in different ways.

THEY SET YOU FREE

A church in a town with a school for the blind had for many years opened its second through fifth grades to the school. The woman in charge was, in the words of the school, *professional.* Everyone trusted her and no one doubted her. Times and tides changed a good bit, and she moved to Dayton, Ohio. Two people took her place with fear and trembling. She wrote to them: "I'll give you my secrets. It is more important that you have them than that I keep them. Guide the blind child by putting your hand on his elbow and remember, above all, that he is a *person* who just happens to be blind. That's all I know that's different from what it takes to teach sighted children. Oh, yes, don't keep changing the furniture around, and keep the place clean."

The information freed the two newcomers. It was not what the woman said, but it was her attitude toward her job that taught them how to get on with theirs.

Everyone isn't that generous, but seldom are veteran teachers intentionally mean. Sometimes they're scared that you won't figure out their code. This is particularly true with teachers of children in first grade and under. So much depends on relationships, attitudes, and the freedom a child has to explore and discover his new surroundings. Adults unfamiliar with education of young children may infer that nothing is being taught when, indeed, the children are learning second by second at a breakneck speed. When a child is three years old, he has been on earth thirty-six months. How much, by comparison, have you learned in the last thirty-six months?

Reading curriculum materials and talking with preschool and first-grade teachers will help you become familiar with what *can* happen and what *does.* Some of the best and surely some of the worst teaching is done with young children.

THEY SET YOUR TEETH ON EDGE

There are those experienced teachers who feign cooperation for their own reasons, generally centered about the fear that you want things done differently and they know only their own ways. Sometimes these men and women are among those who don't prepare or who observe tedious rituals making preparing unnecessary. And at other times, they truly don't know if they're capable or not.

There is a near-famous performance going on weekly in a small church in the South, the facts of which have been reported fairly accurately over the years. What goes on is so outlandish and meaningless that it takes more than an average imagination to fabricate further. Ministers have come and gone; superintendents have shaken their heads, argued, cajoled, and resigned. But the captain runs a tight ship.

She is advancing in years and not losing much energy in the process. She holds session with all boys and girls under fourth grade. They sit on tiny enameled pews. They observe birthdays with a make-believe cake, bank, song, and "cat-echism" concerning party, presents, what they asked for, and what they got. Then they discover who lost teeth this week and generally only the older ones have. They find out what the Good Fairy's rates are and hope the tiny ones don't take to pulling teeth for material gain. Offering is taken, much of it from the floor by this time. Then there is a march. A boy—always a boy—carries the flag of the country. Maybe he can go anywhere he wants to, or perhaps there is a way of knowing the route. The pianist plays "America" and the children follow the Red, White, and Blue until the two-year-olds "fall out" and are taken to a table to color on 4″ x 6″ cards. The boy continues to lead the others in and out of cubicles until they have all had quite enough exercise. The pianist stops the music. The school children hear a Bible story. All others color. They don't draw; they color. When the story is over for the school-age children, they all scamper back to the pews and sing songs "until your parents come."

In the same church a fifth-grade class of boys and girls drew a series of long murals depicting important events in the life of Jesus, learned ten hymns of the church by heart, and sang as a choir in one of the services of worship. When asked to sing again they wrote a letter to the minister saying: "Mr. Barkmann has taught us that a choir does not show off. We will sing in church if everyone else sings with us. We voted on this, because Mr. Barkmann made us tell you what *we* think."

Mr. Barkmann never became the myth the older lady did. He moved out of the small town, and only those fifth-graders knew what it was like to learn and enjoy learning in the church school.

WORK WHERE IT COUNTS

We can't do much with rigid leadership, unwilling to change, and it is probably wise to work in those areas first where people have ears to hear and eyes to see. Occasionally, by contrast, an old soldier will be pressed into changing or quitting. More often he quits; it's not easy to move from accomplishing nothing exactly the same way each week to responding to the five senses of curious, intelligent boys and girls.

It isn't the old among us who cannot change; it is the rigid and the fearful of any age. There is a woman of well over seventy working with teachers of children under six. She is proud, and well she might be. The teachers are doing a consistently good job by contemporary standards in early childhood education.

There is a young woman in that same church who was observed by the pastor one Sunday, because he had heard by way of an ecumenical grapevine that she was an excellent teacher. He went into her fourth-grade class. She had a partner who was watching only; it was her quiz show. Every child confessed his sins on his knees, begged *her* for forgiveness, and then she prayed for his *salvation*. The pastor admitted to the Christian education committee afterward: "I welcomed seeing her teach. Then I was angry. Finally, I left and went to my study and cried." The committee dismissed her from teaching. They said, as generous laymen often do, that perhaps she would be happier and more useful teaching in another church. The minister, still bruised from Sunday's fray, said he surely hoped that no church would welcome such cruelty in teaching the saving love of Christ.

WHY THE BAD EXAMPLES?

With new teachers, the more good examples we can show and tell about, the better their attitudes will be. They teach one class with or without a partner, and we want them to do as well as they can. We probably help them more than the experienced, because they either ask for it or act like they want help.

With new administrators, whether you have been teachers first or not, no holds are barred. It is your job to know the quality and kind of teaching in each class, and if you can, to do something about what should be changed. We'll talk about what can be changed and how to do it without being an underhanded sneak, to put it bluntly. We also have to make very sure that you know the importance of being informed about the methods and techniques of every teacher.

There are administrators who tolerate little variation from what the rest of us call *dead* center. Dead center is not the aim of this book. There are many good but unconventional ways of being a teacher and a pupil, and administrators support both individuals and exist in their jobs for both. Each of us draws a line beyond which he is intolerant for better or worse reasons. The pastor who watched the public confessional had theological, educational, and humanitarian reasons for not tolerating that kind of teaching in the church he served.

Sometimes, and we'll stop and talk about the point of intolerance now, knowing what is going on can be of more educational value to the students than dismissing the teacher and finding a new one.

A director of Christian education kept a journal, she

called it, in which she recorded the episode about a sixth-grade teacher who disturbed the children. The pupils were all girls. Boys asked too many questions, it said. A very intelligent, emotional girl came to her office to complain.

POLLY: I'm so disgusted. I'm so mad. I'm so tired. I'm so mixed up.

D.C.E.: What do you think made you that way?

POLLY: You ready? I blew it. I told Mrs. Etcher I didn't dig Jesus *Christ*. She didn't even ask what I meant. She said: "If that's the kind of girl you are, I don't want you here. I am a failure as a teacher, if that's what you think. Haven't you been listening?"

D.C.E.: What did you mean, Polly?

POLLY: Oh, David and I talked about it, and we came in to talk with you while you were in Chicago.

D.C.E.: Well, now I'm not.

POLLY: But I'm saying that's why I told her, because I didn't talk to you.

D.C.E.: So! Talk to me.

POLLY: I read that book by Norman Langford. It was easy and it was hard too. He keeps a mystery story going about Jesus. And I think there *is* a mystery about him. He's not like I am or my dad or my brother David. He may not even have started out that way. But he's not the stupid spook Mrs. Etcher says he is.

D.C.E.: She didn't say he was a stupid spook, did she?

POLLY: No. She said he was the Christ. And I said, "What do you mean, Christ?" And she said the Messiah and God's Son, and the Anointed, I think—just garbage.

D.C.E.: Oh, Polly, come on! I like those words!

POLLY: The way she said them! She didn't answer me. She gave me words but not answers.

D.C.E.: So what do you think of Jesus?

POLLY: Well, David and I talked to Daddy. It was a big thing, you know. And Daddy's like you—he asks questions. So we told him that Jesus was good enough for us just being what he was. He healed people because they believed he was healing for God. It isn't—like David said—as if we're atheists. So then we came to Easter, and I said Jesus would be just as alive if he hadn't risen, because he's *real*. But David said there must have been something to the empty tomb, and Daddy said, "When you cats are over forty, you'll look at Polly's *real* a little differently." I like it when adults dare me on those things. I'm sure I'll remember when I'm forty. I'm that kind.

D.C.E.: Let's get back to Mrs. Etcher. I can talk to her about what you said to me and your dad.

POLLY: She disturbs the other girls too.

D.C.E.: How?

POLLY: I shouldn't say that. They're not my friends. They just look funny sometimes. They're peculiar anyway. They talk to their mothers.

D.C.E.: So do I. Now, back to Mrs. Etcher.

POLLY: Well, I know what you want to know. I'll go back to class. If she makes me mad, I'll come in here, but I'll wait. Okay? I know what I believe now. I may change. I kind of hope I do, so that I can think about it more. The neatest thing about religion is thinking about it.

D.C.E.: Yes. I like to think. But I like to think about what I *believe*.

POLLY: When I'm old I'll probably be that way too.

D.C.E.: You've made my week, Polly! I may never make it to the mailbox for my pension check in 1994.

POLLY: Don't panic. David and I will bring it to your lawn chair!

A conversation like this is worth the time. This intelligent sixth-grader, with fortification from home, was not typical of her classmates. She was not likely to hear any other classmate challenge the teacher. Probably, the teacher should not continue, but that is another problem. While she does, it is that director's business to see that nothing *morbid* happens in class.

To repeat, even though you just read it: *you must see what is going on in the church school* to avoid unfortunate or, worse yet, irretrievable situations. You can't see and hear through closed doors. We have been accused, and justifiably, of causing guilt feelings in young children. For the most part, it has not been the church's stance, but the "sermon" from the classroom that raised the guilt issue. Had the supervisors and administrators been on their guard, facts would have been known, at least, and some events might have been altered or never gotten off the drawing board.

CHANGE WITH HASTE AND CAUTION

Because your eyes are new to the situation, it is more than likely that you'll see places where changes should be made or should have been made years ago. Before you hear yourself telling someone, "Something must be done about . . . ," go through this simple mental exercise. Think of at least three possible ways to go about changing what you feel is ineffective or unwholesome. Think of each person involved and how your separate solutions will affect him. After that exercise, you may be able to present your means of change to the necessary committee or persons instead of your criticism of what went on before you came.

It is most difficult to listen to a criticism of one's own work, no matter how deserving the bad notices are. It is less painful by far to listen to new ideas designed to take the place of the old ones.

Some words of warning on the source and form of ideas for change are appropriate here. There are two places to get innovative notions about administration and organization of an educational program: (1) from others and (2) from your own mind.

Ideas from others come from books, magazines, teacher education courses, and church school leaders who like to brag. The important thing to remember about what you read or hear is that it was reported by one person, very likely put together by a committee, and almost certainly put into effect by a great many more people. If it appears to be the answer to one of your problems, you can be sure that it will need adjusting and modifying in order to fit your school's needs, and that it will be adjusted and modified more before it starts to work for you.

A good many years ago a modest, somewhat timid woman initiated a parent education program in the church in which she worked. It was a middle-sized church in a middle-sized town in the Middle West. The program was an unqualified success. It was reported on locally, regionally, and alas, nationally, where it was written into a booklet and became the recommended emphasis for the year. Many churches tried it with disappointing results. Some churches modified it with better results. Two churches were so enthusiastic they wanted to continue the program and help other parents organize in other churches. Upon close examination, the first church reporting success was in a town devoted to the lumber industry and owned by the company. The minister never before had witnessed any all-out effort to make church programs lively or even well attended. The program, however, was run by the parents from and in their homes. The organizers were largely wives of management and foremen. In a company town, is it any wonder that it worked?

The second enthusiastic church was a small, semirural one with an imaginative pastor and people who enjoyed getting together for a number of reasons. It was not a community, hectic with civic organizations. Even the school was not the center of activity that the church was. The minister's comment in his summary was: "Almost anything works here if it means getting together. Our problem is making the get-togethers worthwhile."

The lumber community had adopted the program because it was recommended nationally. We do not know how many other churches used so slim a reason. The semirural church selected the program because the parents felt that they had common concerns to talk over with one another.

Any program developed nationally must be adapted to individual church needs and used at a time when it does the church the most good. There is no predictable, packaged program available and guaranteed to help everyone with everything all the time.

Ideas you make up yourself may be old or new, born of experience, or dreamed up at the kitchen sink. You may be new in your job in the church in which you're working, but a veteran from somewhere else. Even if you have time-tested ideas from elsewhere, discuss them with others before you expect them to be adopted just the way you brought them along. Most program ideas are ways to improve what we are and what we have, and in each church what people are and have differ from any other church.

A young man, whose job made it necessary for him to move every two or three years, was a senior high adviser in several churches. He was highly esteemed and rather widely known for at least ten years. It was a total surprise, as you can imagine, to the minister of one of the first churches he worked in to find him in the city jail, addicted to drugs, divorced, and without a job.

"My job and my work at church were alike," he explained to his former pastor. "I had a bag of tricks, and everywhere I did the same thing, over and over. The materials we used always stressed planning with the young people. But those were *my* ideas we used and they carried them out. The spaghetti supper all over town, the car wash in the Square, the clothing drive for hippies. . . . It was a drag—a preoccupation with meaninglessness. Everywhere the same. How can you stand it, Pastor?"

The young man, now in his early thirties, had tired of his own programs and had not been free enough to let them be adapted in each church in which he served. The posters for publicity, the letters written to the young people, the parent involvement, and the total absence of any participation in the life of the rest of the church had changed remarkably little from the first to the last church in which he worked. It is no wonder he was bored with his program's meaninglessness; but he was riding a treadmill of his own making, going nowhere while the earth beneath him moved.

Whenever you work with an idea from your mind or your experience elsewhere, it is imperative that you consult the veterans on the team, not just to feel them out for their disposition to change, but to get their counsel from their years of experience and time spent in a church that is still new to you.

You may hear, "We tried that once, and it didn't work." We all say that, knowing full well that we deserve to be asked: "When? Why didn't it work? How did you go about it? Who was involved?" Ask those questions of veterans; they've been expecting them for years. What insults them most is a lack of curiosity about their past, because it robs them of their reputation for uniqueness. And every church community is unique.

RECKONING WITH UNIQUENESS

It takes a sensitivity most of us don't possess to be able to discover the uniqueness of a church we've just begun to work in or have just started attending. That takes knowing people, watching them work, hearing about their past as a people of God, and working for a good while with them.

It takes no sensitivity at all to accept the fact of uniqueness and to *run with patience* in a quest for exactly what that fact involves.

A very large suburban church had for years resembled a country church grown big, rather than an institution with a program for every age, a choir for every child, and, incidentally, worship on Sunday. With the high rate of mobility in that suburb, weekly visitors came, went, and some came back to be members and to work in the church school. Time after time a new administrator, capable from having served in other churches, brought up the appalling lack of both organization and meetings. Seldom did one mention a criticism of the teaching he saw.

The director of children's work, fairly new herself, used to explain: "This isn't a meet-together church. This is a no-nonsense, get-the-job-done church. *Our* job is to help those teachers who ask for help, support those who are doing a good job, and try everything under the sun to help those who don't think they need us."

The organization was there; it consisted of paths not hurdles, handrails not ditches. Everyone didn't have to use the same roadways to get where he was going. New ways were made for new people. If a group of teachers wanted to meet regularly, they did. When two of them preferred to use the telephone or stop by the church to plan, no one was surprised. There were "meetings" all over town; they just didn't make headlines in the church bulletin.

A word of caution must be sounded about attempting such an intricate, yet freewheeling system of working with people, many of whom thrive in such a situation. Those who are in charge of the education and well-being of teachers *must know each one well*. They must know how well he gets along with those he teaches, those he teaches with, and what he teaches too. You cannot make roads and pathways with those people you don't know. The roads won't lead anywhere.

Another word to those courageous enough to try working with persons, one at a time: *you must follow through.*

38

That's what "being there" is all about. No veteran is dull-witted enough not to see the difference between ideas that might work and those which are in operation.

A superintendent of a small village church decided after a painful but rather healing operation of a year's use of new church school materials that no teacher could resign until he had talked with his replacement about what he'd learned about unit teaching and session-planning. One of the men who was leaving town said, "Al, that's a good idea, but first let's talk to one another to find out if we knew what we were doing this year." They did, and they found out that, although there were similarities in understanding, practices varied greatly from age group to age group.

"Maybe," said Al, "we ought to get together once a month and plan our units together." The women from the kindergarten shrieked, and one said: "You mean you'd like to help us plan when to bake cookies and make apple-sauce for the shut-ins? That's what *we* do!" There was good feeling in the group, and because there was, one of the kindergarten teachers said: "We're talking five different languages, and all we're saying is that we have different objectives. *We* know why we make applesauce. Do you know why you study the Gospel of Mark? Or teach the kids how to use a concordance?" It cleared the air and the mud from the path. They went back to Al's original idea, better prepared to work with new teachers. Al was a good bit better informed himself on what was involved in teaching different age groups and why.

Don't underestimate the veterans. Be grateful they're working with you and you with them. They can welcome new teachers and help them in very specific ways. That's what we'll talk about next.

scouting for and training the rookies

It may not be your job to get new teachers each year, but if you know someone who wants to teach, it's a cinch he'll be considered. Give his name and information about him to the person or committee in your organization who enlists help for the church school.

If it is your job to fill vacancies in your teaching staff, here are six rules of thumb to encourage you.

THE TEACHERS ARE THERE

Rule of Thumb No. 1

You have many adults in your church, and surely more than enough to replace the entire church school staff, although the thought is a depressing one. Do you know all of them by name? Do you know something about each one —like what he did in a former church, what he does in the community, what line of work he's in, or if he is a former day school teacher? Chances are you don't, unless your church is small or you grew up in your big one.

Your job is to find and find out about people you may never have met. Probably the most efficient way, heaven forbid, is to form a committee to scout for teachers. It works best to have people from various age groups, organizations, and boards so that together you are likely to know every person in the church. At the first meeting, go through the entire church membership list together and record any person's recommendation. If a member of the church is unknown to everyone there, except the minister who received him as a parishioner, record his name too. He may not make a good teacher, but he surely needs a call from someone soon if no one knows him at all.

Now you have a list from which your teachers will probably come. If the committee was chosen well and has done a thorough job, it may never have to meet again. Your scouting begins now.

YOU HAVE TO ASK THEM TO TEACH

Rule of Thumb No. 2

There are more than enough clever gimmicks for getting teachers that are written step by step in books you can easily find. They vary from asking parents to visit their children's classes so that someone can decide if they look like teachers to having the superintendent make a broadcast appeal from the pulpit on Christian Education Sunday. The former is called parent contact when in reality it is sneaky scouting for teachers. The latter is called a sermon on Christian education and boils down to: "Come on all you folks out there. Anyone can teach!"

Well, anyone can't. All you have to do is try it that way

and watch. You're not filling post office boxes with "Occupant" mail; you're looking for someone who, with help, can teach a specific group of children, young people, or adults. There is nothing wrong with parental visits to the classroom, if they're intended to share with the parents what kinds of work their offspring engage in at church. Surely, once a year, if the superintendent is inclined, his views on Christian education should be heard, because his vantage point is unlike anyone else's in the church. But let's not get our motives confused. The very least we can be in the church is honest with one another.

So ask individuals, one at a time. They have the option of saying yes or no. For that reason, begin less abruptly than, "Could you teach the seventh-graders?" (Only a small minority in all Christendom would say yes to that one on first encounter with a stranger.)

You might say to a lady on your list, "Mrs. Gregory of the Women's Association suggested you as a person who might like to teach church school next year." Then you find out, sometimes spontaneously, that the lady has or has not taught before, may have been a day school teacher but never taught church school, or is a recent convert to Christianity. You may hear a lot of excuses, too, but that's another rule of thumb all its own. The point here is that as you engage in conversation you find out many things about the person, and determine tentatively what age group and situation would best fit. Does she seem to need the help of a strong lead teacher in a group teaching situation? Is she likely to want to teach by herself? Can she teach at only one time of the year? Would she be a candidate for substituting at a particular age level?

Record immediately what actual information you have found out and what your initial hunches are. Even if the lady gives an adamant no, write it down; you won't have to ask her next year.

You may not enjoy the encounters at first, largely because you'll be afraid of being turned down. On the whole, as you look back after the job is finished, you will be surprised at how many more people you know in the church and what common, ordinary fine folks they are, whether they want to teach or not. With practice, you'll improve your own calling techniques, unlike anyone else's. You'll learn what times to call during the day or evening, and above all when in the course of the church year to make the first contact.

YOU HAVE TO ASK THEM SOON ENOUGH
Rule of Thumb No. 3

One of the reasons the superintendent makes his plea to any and all souls on Christian Education Sunday is that those who were in charge of getting teachers met in August and called when most prospects were out of town or committed to a busy year of volunteering in other areas of their lives.

April is about the time of year when other organizations in your community begin to ask their workers to return for another year and to look for replacements for those not returning. April is far enough from September so that the time a job takes doesn't loom over an already busy person. He can think about the job sensibly—if he knows what it is.

Part of knowing what the job is consists of settling on the precise age group with whom the person will be working. That you can decide on in April and May.

Next he will need to know with whom he will be working. Is there a coordinator, a lead teacher, a teammate? What are their names? You won't always have all vacancies filled that early, and you should be frank in admitting that your attempts so far have not brought forth a colleague for the person who has agreed to teach. He may know of someone he can tell you about. (It is not his job to ask; you were given that one. In the event that you call the person, it's simply: "Hal Emerson is going to teach fifth-graders next year. He thinks it would be fun to have you as a teammate. What do you think?")

And most important, he will need all his materials so that he can scan, read, and study them over the summer. Someone in the administration of the school or department in which he teaches should give him a walk-through of all the materials given to him. A walk-through can be part of the orientation we'll discuss later or it can be in the man's living room. Curriculum materials are becoming increasingly bulky per teacher. Guides for teachers, books for pupils, activity packets, filmstrips, records, hymnals, song charts, maps are, believe it, only a few of the resources a teacher might use. The day is gone when you put "it" in an envelope and mailed his quarterly to the new teacher, who sat down after *The Lone Ranger* was over and read his "lesson" for the first day on the job.

He'll need to know right away that you expect him to have questions and that there will be a time for him to meet with someone who can answer them. It's crucial to follow through on promises like this. He has time to give up before he starts if no one helps him. Everyone needs the help of others with present-day materials. They are intended for group planning from the very beginning.

Find out when he intends to be gone or too busy to meet so that the person or persons who are in charge of orientation of new teachers can be sure of an appropriate time.

And, finally, let him know as soon as it is known what students will be in his class, where they live, and to whom they belong if they're children. (It may not be difficult to find the father of George Eugene Hammersley, Jr., but Mary Jones's is a whole new problem.)

One of the ways you can reflect the gratitude of the church for the service he has agreed to offer is to be sure that your system of calling, handing out material and information, and invitations to an orientation works like greased lightning. Check and recheck with other leaders throughout the summer so that no one is abandoned and no one has that excuse to abandon the job.

YOU CAN ELIMINATE MANY EXCUSES
Rule of Thumb No. 4

There is a distinct difference between an excuse and a reason for not teaching. The reasons are true and unchangeable. Even "Because I don't want to" may be a reason, and not a bad one at that. Excuses are ways of weaseling out, and it's up to you to decide which excuses you will accept and which ones you will try to eliminate. Eliminating excuses helps you determine whether the person is interested enough to become a teacher in spite of his initial reservations. Eliminating excuses may improve your church school, because inherent in every knocked-down excuse is a promise from the church.

The excuses fall into these general categories:

"I don't know how" may be telling the truth. Whether he can learn or not is a matter for your discernment. Tell him what opportunities there are for learning to teach before and during the time he teaches. If he can't possibly come to meetings beforehand—another excuse —you might mention that his experienced *teammate* might work with him at their mutual convenience. If he wants to teach, he's likely to say yes at the mention of an able-bodied teacher in the classroom with him. If he still resists, perhaps you should let him.

"But I've never taught before" may turn out to have been an education major in college who, though never having taught, did learn something about how to go about it. You might mention that a high percentage of the church school teachers who are enjoying their work and doing it well had a first day themselves. Again, offer the support of your system for fledgling teachers. Be specific,

45

and point out that there is plenty of time to prepare before the first day and there are lots of learning opportunities while on the job. A person with this excuse may need only your encouragement and the choice of several jobs in several age groups. He or she will probably work best in cooperation with a capable teacher or a group as is found in most preschool sections.

"I'm out of town a good bit" may be gone no more than many commuters. He forgets that on Friday nights he generally comes home, and that he can study his church school material in motel rooms, on long plane rides, and in rent-a-car lines. If he really is gone some weekends, he needs to be teaching with a partner or a group. And if he's teaching with a partner, let it not be a weak sister. She has to be fully capable of carrying through what was begun and initiating what is to come. We're way past pairing up Horace Mann with King Kong and thinking we have two teachers.

If it's not work but play that takes him out of town, you may have to settle on the teaching of one course in a senior high or adult class. If he skis, try fall and late spring for a six weeks' series. If he sails, winter might yield more small craft warnings and keep him in town. But if he says he sails and skis, believe him; it's a reason.

"Well, I always say, once you get in, you can't get out" should be reminded immediately that you asked her (generally) for only a year and you meant it. After all, you may decide, a year is plenty! Sometimes the excuse is based on history in some church, if not yours. Surely no one who decides not to come back after a year should be made to feel guilty for having worked a year. No one should continue because he feels guilty about quitting. And anyone who finds teaching an art and wants to continue should be welcome to do so for as long as he wishes.

If your reminder doesn't bring forth an affirmative answer, she may offer one of the other excuses. If you want her services enough, follow the guidelines under those excuses.

Don't tease. If you can't persuade someone with honest offers, shake the dust off your feet and go on to the next one. It is better to have ten inexperienced, eager, curious Christians in the process of learning how to teach than forty experienced, bored, reluctant teachers who are doing you a personal favor by being there.

YOU SHOULD NOT ACCEPT SOME PEOPLE
Rule of Thumb No. 5

We said that everyone can't teach. It is also true that some should not. Some of the people recommended to you are suggested because of a particular interest the committee member has in the person. For specific reasons he may not be good for your school or your school may not be the best thing for him. Here are a few examples; you will find more.

"I don't like your curriculum materials, but I have lots of ideas myself." This kind of person is worth listening to. One out of a thousand, to be generous, has better ideas about education in the church than the makers and shapers of your materials. If he can tell you what kinds of things he doesn't like about the materials, you may find yourself agreeing with him. Here take caution. The important qualification for his teaching with such an attitude is that he can also tell you what he would put *in* the classroom instead. Many of the teachers who are bound to senseless rituals or harangues disturbing to their pupils began with an objection to the materials.

It well may be that the church should study the possibility of changing its curriculum materials, but it is not for you to decide on the spot that the objector should teach without them. Every series of curriculum materials constitutes a system. What is done in third-graders' materials depends somewhat on what came before and what is to follow. If you explain that much, it will be evident that the person is not being asked to bring only his opposition to the classroom.

In recording the person's response, you might give his name to those people who are responsible for choice of materials. Besides hearing his opinions, they may be able to use his mind on a reexamination of the materials that are used. All people who oppose the use of certain printed resources are not bigots. Some are well-informed educators and theologians.

"I am a new Christian. I was a lapsed Jew before I was married." This individual may be very intelligent and more curious about the faith than some persons now teaching. He may become a very good teacher eventually because he is curious and understands the mind of one who is hearing the story of Jesus Christ for the first time. There are many places for such a person to serve in the church, but it is most likely that the time for teaching should be postponed until he has satisfied himself that he is more knowledgeable about the Christian faith.

People from other faiths are leaven in our midst. Young people might use them as resource people in courses of church history or comparative contemporary religions.

Adult study groups might want to use them as discussion leaders in their particular religious field. A man who for many years has been a Presbyterian grew up in a Pentecostal community. He was a Christian when he became a Presbyterian, but the two churches were very different. He was asked to teach and he refused. "I want to be a student for a while. You folks use your minds so differently from what I'm used to," he said. He was a favorite of the adult class, because of his disarming manner of asking basic questions about Biblical interpretation. The others found themselves examining their own statements more carefully than before he joined them. New Christians and even new Presbyterians need some time to be students before they are expected to be teachers.

"I don't belong to any church, but since my children go here, I suppose I should help out." It's a temptation to accept so kind an offer, especially if you are perilously close to the bottom of your list. But the church school offers education that ultimately helps the student be a responsible *member* of the church. Here again a senior high or adult class might call upon such a person *because* he is not a member of any church. Being against membership in the institution and sending one's children to its school is a position young people and adults might enjoy discussing together.

A director of Christian education tells about interviewing a man who had said that he would teach sixth grade but that he was not a church member. He said, "You don't tell them Jesus walked on water, do you?"

"Oh, yes, they read the Gospels," she answered.

"And that David had long hair and Bathsheba cut it?"

"No. Samson and Delilah," she told him.

"You're an intelligent person otherwise. Where did you go wrong?"

"Oh, back there in seventh grade," she replied, "when a teacher questioned our facts as well as our beliefs. I started reading the Bible and books about the Bible."

The man did not teach sixth grade that year. He started reading the Bible and books about the Bible. He and the minister became close friends. He joined the church and before serving on the official board taught sixth grade.

"She's just come from the mental hospital, and she needs to get involved." There are many ways church members can support the convalescing mental patient. Being sensitive to when he needs people and when he'd sooner be without them is one way. Always being there, when he needs someone or another. Teaching church school at any level takes a great deal of energy. It takes knowing

49

who you are as a person so that you are not afraid of the student or of other adults. If normal, healthy minds avoid failure, think how important it is that these persons should be in situations where they succeed.

There are other jobs in the church for people recovering from mental illnesses. Some of the service rendered by the church involves working with other adults on specific short-lived projects—things that get finished before one's eyes. Try those things first. Don't put a sick man in a room by himself to catalog old books or worse yet, to dust them. That job is almost intolerable to most of us; otherwise it would have been done years ago.

After a while, if the person likes to be with young children, he or she may serve adequately as an assistant in the nursery or kindergarten. Children are unpredictable in their behavior and in their attitudes toward adults. With other adults present as buffers, chance remarks need not cut so deeply as they might.

In one church, a woman who was an outpatient at a mental hospital worked as an assistant with two excellent nursery teachers. She was overweight and under sedation and sat down a good bit. The children brought books for her to read and generally "played" with her. One morning as she left, a man picking up his son whispered to the teachers, "Who's *that?*" His son answered, "Oh, that's my good old fat lady!"

Factors vary so much in mental health disorders that we cannot generalize. Sensitivity to and knowledge of the person and his illness are essential. He can truly be needed without teaching a class.

YOU MUST DELIVER ON YOUR PROMISES

Rule of Thumb No. 6

When you say "We will help you," and the promise is fulfilled, the reputation of the school gets around. People are more willing to volunteer when they are assured that they don't have to go it alone. Just knocking down their excuses with promises showed them that someone was listening to their answers.

Making good on promises involves the whole ball club and simple enough organization so that at any given moment the participants know how near they are to their individual goals. Reporting and checking are what make your system work. If you are getting teachers, you report to the people who give the teachers their materials, to whoever is in charge of assigning classes, and to those who are arranging orientation. They in turn check with you and one another. It's a person-to-person ball game, and to stay ahead you have to work out a signal system.

"You can work with an experienced teacher" calms the nerves of a neophyte educator. It requires sizing up both the new teacher and an experienced one so that the two will have a chance of being compatible. Team teaching is neither good nor bad in itself. It is, at its worst, a way of assuring the administration that the class will be manned each Sunday. At its best it is a combination of personalities that makes each one's contribution more valuable because of the other one's. Sometimes it is supportive to the new teacher to watch an able educator at work. It is almost always more helpful to the beginner if the partner assists him in participation so that he becomes more adept by doing some teaching himself.

Planning with the partner from the beginning is of as much value as teaching with him. One of the main reasons for poor teaching is not knowing how to plan and not understanding the importance of thorough planning. The more complicated a set of materials teachers have, the more essential it is that they plan together for optimum use of the books and other resources.

"We will teach you some of the skills before you begin" generally means a workshop. A workshop may be as in-

volved as a day at the church with tables and tables filled with raw materials for puppets, dioramas, murals, slide shows, and classroom scrapbooks. It may be one experienced teacher with two beginners learning about tempera, finger paint, and crayon resist at her kitchen table and sink. Workshops are where work is done. Learning about drama or discussion by dramatizing or discussing constitutes a workshop.

To save everyone time and energy, find out from the new recruits what kinds of skills they need to practice. There is no point in making preparations for a project everyone knows how to do. There is negative value in it only; it tells the people right away that meetings aren't necessary.

"We will introduce the materials to you and help you find answers to your questions" is essential before the teachers begin. You may be able to arrange for several teachers to work with a group of new ones so that many questions are aired and answered. Planning a unit and a first session might familiarize them with the function of each piece of material. Just showing everything and talking about it is not too helpful. Almost anyone can figure that much out. New teachers need to know: How much is given? What do I have to think up myself? Where is the plan written down? Where are the directions? How long does it take the boys and girls to do what I have planned? How do I plan with them and still use the guidebook?

The new teachers will be relieved to know that any materials take some getting used to and that working with the books and other resources during the year will gradually turn their strangeness to familiarity.

"We have no one else teaching fifth grade, but we'll introduce you to someone from St. Andrew's Church who is using the same materials we are." With all the emphasis on getting along with other denominations and faiths,

we often forget to cooperate with our sister churches within our denomination. In fact, we compete. It is helpful to attend one another's meetings for all teachers or a few teachers. It is even more helpful to offer service back and forth, not available in both churches.

Very few churches have strong, able leadership throughout the school and could profit by a sharing back and forth—a pooling of leaders in a most informal way. Leaders of leaders have been around for years, but they have worked, generally, through a district office. They are useful godsends, and their number could surely be increased to include those people who are available by phone when the time comes for planning a unit or working out a sticky problem in the classroom.

These are some of the promises and ways to make them work for you. They all say, "We care." With this amount of help available at the beginning, some of the standard church school problems are not likely to develop. When some do, you want to be very sure the lines of communication are open.

One way to keep conversations going with the teachers is to visit their classrooms, sometimes early, before the pupils are there in great number. Visit for an entire session later in the year. And no matter what you see, what went wrong, what needs to be corrected immediately, *never* leave the room without a word of encouragement.

PLUGGING THE HOLES

As the year goes on, vacancies may occur in the teaching staff. This is not so serious if you have teams of teachers working together, because you can more easily find a person to help than one to take over. Probably your most valuable resource for "filling in" is a veteran on sabbatical rather than a rookie. Remember how much orientation you offered before the new ones started in September? Do you have that kind of time to spend now? If you do, the inexperienced person will fare as well as any of the others did.

Good substitutes may see you through the rest of the year or until a rookie has had orientation. With young people's or adult classes, you may be able to find several people to teach short courses of four to six sessions. The man who skis and the one who thinks he's out of town too often may well be adequate replacements.

Many times young people themselves want to teach. They are excellent helpers with young children if they have done a good bit of baby-sitting and if the leadership in charge is dedicated to teaching them how to work with groups. Teaching should not be a reason to forgo what is available for their age group, but it can be of value in the choice of one's vocation.

A pediatrics nurse in one church has done most constructive work as supervisor of crib babies, toddlers, and two-year-olds. Her assistants have been junior highs and senior highs along with adults. She is conscious of teaching them all the time. They learn the difference between a "mad" cry and a "sad" cry. They learn when to interfere and when to let two children settle their differences with two-year-old minds. They learn that soft voices beget soft voices. And above all, they learn that in the Christian community the patience with which they have been treated they pass on to the children.

Young people are particularly welcome in any age group where they can accompany singing with a guitar, flute, or piano. The singing may stop momentarily as the pupils watch a boy playing his guitar, but very soon they are singing with him. One of your goals might be having a singing church school. Instruments, including the magnificent human voice, can furnish the accompaniment young voices need in learning to sing.

When, upon rare occasions, the young person is in charge for a session, one of the administrators, at least, should know it and check in now and then to encourage and to help, if necessary. With young children, not even an adult should be by himself for too long.

The magic words with fledglings, as with all of us who teach, from you are: "We support you and we care about you."

where
you're going
and why

Every good coach knows that a winning team cannot rely on only one good player. It takes the high morale of everyone involved to win again and again. Each one is assured of the other's contributions and thereby is more useful himself. The minute we start having star players we're in trouble. When the coaches and managers think the team won't run without them, they're surprised. And when the general manager, if we dare call the minister that, thinks he's calling all the plays, he finds out it's a physical impossibility, not to mention a psychological one. People aren't automatons, and in the church a person is not a series of numbers.

HOPES, AIMS, AND GOALS

Churches have *hopes* for the education of their young. They hold church school classes at which the learners talk, listen, sing, read the Bible, dramatize, and sometimes color, cut out, paste, and put up pictures. Presumably, these activities embody *aims* at some sort of *goal*.

Let's say that a teacher's goal is instant conversion to what he considers model behavior. The way in which he aims for it is to frighten seven-year-olds with a god who knows exactly what behavior is expected at Trinity-Post Road Federated Church and a devil who has his own expressway open to hell in a brand-new, battery-operated dune buggy.

This aim and the intended target may not be the hope at all of church education in that congregation. Only a chance remark from a worried child, at best, or the bad dream from a hysterical one may inform those who should care most about aims and targets concerning the younger generation.

The goal may be, instead, to get through the hour, and the aim may be to talk about summer vacations until then. It is doubtful that the congregation had that in mind either. They went into debt for the building, ordered the curriculum materials, and had the last appreciation dinner for teachers and leaders in the church school. Surely they deserve more for their efforts than idle conversation for an hour.

DETERMINING GOALS

If you've never sat down to determine precise goals for church education, you might well wonder how a whole congregation goes about it.

The first key word is *representative* and the second is *small*. Begin with a small, representative group. You can plan as elaborately or as simply as you wish in order to get the job done. The example of one church that follows is elaborate. The group went to a member's summer home for two and a half days and did very little else but determine goals, eat, and play volley ball. You might want to devote several evenings or Saturday afternoons to the same project. The advantages of being together for a prolonged time are that the same people are at all meetings, there are few distractions, no review of previous meetings is necessary, and there is a terminal point at which the job must be finished.

HOW ONE CHURCH DID IT

A church of slightly over six hundred members with one pastor and an assistant in Christian education from the congregation planned a meeting of the following leaders:

the minister
the assistant in Christian education
three members of the official board
the superintendent of the church school
six representatives from teaching staff
one parent who did not teach
the area Christian education man, who came because
    he thought they meant business.

There were fourteen people, about one fortieth of the congregation.

The questions they came to answer were deceptively simple:

What do we want our Christian education program
    to accomplish?
How can we get what we want?
How will we know we have accomplished anything?
    Or won't we?

Those were the three (or four) questions to be discussed for two and a half days. The administrators met in one group and the teachers with the parent met in another. They used their denominational curriculum materials for general guidance and departed from them to make what they called local adaptations.

For two hours each group discussed the first question and then came together for a progress report, which turned out to be a confession of ignorance. The administrators knew very little about age differences and consequent program variations. One of the women from the official board had been an early childhood educator before she was married. She said wryly that to talk about education to her co-workers was as fruitless as speaking fluent Turkish to a London hotel clerk. One of the men had answered the first question by saying, "We want to teach the Bible to the older ones and let the little ones play." The woman was indignant.

The teachers confessed that they didn't know what went on and what was emphasized in departments other than their own, and the parent said he had always figured the teachers knew what they were doing.

The fourteen voted to stay together during the afternoon session and asked the minister, the assistant in Christian education, and the superintendent to constitute a panel to inform the rest of them on general principles of education in the church. It was a difficult assignment, and while the others ate and played volley ball, the three panel members ate and planned their program.

The assistant in Christian education told what kinds of things were planned for children and young people because of their age and development. She explained why three-year-olds need more room per person than adults do, why elementary-age children work on art projects, and why junior highs go on field trips.

The superintendent reviewed the subject matter of the denominational curriculum material for every age group. While he was explaining some of the contemporary issues dealt with Biblically at the junior high level, he stopped abruptly. "By jove, this is ingenious! What Betty said and what I'm saying fit together." That much light at the end of the tunnel made the entire event worthwhile.

The minister spoke bluntly. He said that Christians are people called out to serve Christ. One way is to tell his story in the most effective way we can. Four-year-olds surrounded by Christian teachers learn from the environment that the church is a good place to be. When a child can read, the Book of the church is shared with him. And at whatever age, the meeting of the worshiping congregation is welcome to him. "We are not," he concluded, "running a humdrum Sunday school. It must be a school for Christians."

There were many questions afterward. That evening the administrators and the teachers met again in separate groups. They answered the first question and were in fair agreement from group to group. The second question —How can we get what we want?—was not as easily answered and, therefore, was postponed until the next morning. The mood of the fourteen was one of elation if not silliness by the time they dismissed for an evening snack.

The next day, working together, they made concrete plans for teacher education which included short-term courses in January and May, a visitation program of all classes by the education committee of the official board, and help in session planning by the assistant in Christian education. The minister, the assistant in Christian education, and the early childhood educator from the official board agreed to conduct the short-term courses. The feeling of the entire group was that teacher education was the place to begin.

The minister insisted, along with the area Christian education man, that there were long-range goals as well. The two were labeled visionaries and idealists until they came up with parent education and participation in the work of the church, a well-organized, informed advisory committee for Christian education, and students who could show evidence of having learned what supposedly was taught.

A group of four, working with the area Christian educator, defended the steps in forming and functioning as a Christian education committee.

The minister worked with four others, including the parent, on listing ways in which the whole church could involve parents more significantly than it was. The man representing the parents said that he had always enjoyed parents' days at church school and panels with the young people, but that any meeting called "parent education" was not for him. He asked instead for an open line to the minister at times when his family and his friends needed help. In return, he said, he'd do almost anything short of tying quilts with the ladies on Tuesdays. "You'll have no difficulty getting grateful people to come to worship on Sunday morning," he said.

The assistant in Christian education worked with three teachers on an understanding of specific, *behavioral* objectives. Each objective stated what a student could *do* to demonstrate that he had learned something. Retelling the story of the prodigal son demonstrates that the person remembers the events. Making a modern interpretation of it in drama demonstrates an understanding of the meaning in the parable. They began working out a complicated chart of behavioral objectives at each age level, but abandoned it, as it looked more and more like a hidebound system instead of an aid in teaching. In reporting to the whole group, they defined the term "behavioral objective" and gave examples of behavioral objectives having to do with Biblical content and socialization within a class.

The next morning the fourteen made plans for communicating their findings to the congregation and for meeting again in three months.

Two Sundays later in the bulletin was a list of goals. The congregation was to rate them in importance. "To demonstrate a familiarity with Biblical literature by answering 100 questions" came in first. "To become an active participant in the worship and work of the church" came in last. "Apparently," said the minister, "we've plenty of work to do right here."

The next week the congregation was asked to draw lines through those activities listed which they would like to see used with the children in arriving at their goals. Most of the sheets had lines through everything. An octogenarian who signed his name wrote, "I wish I was a kid these days in this church."

There were no hooks in these unscientific sanctuary games. They were simply an attempt to find out what the congregation thought about aims and goals for church education. The fourteen had just begun their work. They were organized for intelligent participation in a program where the main goal was that everyone in it knew what he was doing and why.

DIFFERENT OBJECTIVES FOR DIFFERENT PEOPLE

A great many things have to happen at the same time in the church. The calendar doesn't stop in order for the school to "get ready." That is probably a blessing, because a year, six months, or even a solid month of nothing but talk of objectives would be tiresome indeed. Besides, good objectives are born of insights that spin off spontaneously from experience. Vacuum-packed objectives grow stale when exposed to the air mortals breathe.

Each working group with one resource person outside of the group can begin by outlining basic objectives or goals. The departmental superintendent or coordinator might be the "outsider" with a group of first-grade teachers or a group of teachers of first through fourth grades. He must be one who is aware of the development of the school's goals and the objectives of the other age groups. He has to have done his homework. It isn't enough to be a good discussion leader, if you've been asked to be resourceful.

Sometimes a whole department is a solid block of opposition to the instructional goals of the school. And sometimes for a variety of rather good reasons you have to live with the conditions. Here is where school goals and church government, whatever yours is, can help you. You can make the school's goals known and bring the opposition out in the open to see it for what it is. If the goals were made, as in the example above, by representatives of the official board with teachers and administrators cooperating, you have solid support for insisting on teamwork.

In a church in the southeast a primary department of first through third grades used materials chosen by the teachers and taught, they claimed, Christ in every lesson. A new general superintendent was appointed in the spring to begin work in the fall. She began visiting classes as soon as she was named. She had a wide-eyed naïve expression on her youthful face and no one was prepared for her articulate descriptions of what she saw in the primary department.

The lead teacher scurried about as the children were arriving, trying to find a set of materials for the superintendent, all the time telling her why they didn't use what the rest of the school did. She found everything but a spare pupil's book. "I had one just last Sunday," she clucked. The young lady spied a booklet under the short leg of a table, picked it up, and was assured that she had indeed found the missing link.

There was a story on the left-hand page and a picture to color on the right. The story told about Solomon's wisdom and zeroed in on the fight the two women had over to whom the baby belonged. In the picture to color, Solomon was holding the baby by his feet and had a long, menacing butcher knife in his other hand, poised for action. The women hid behind their headgear in horror. Christ in every lesson?

The session progressed, much to the superintendent's delight, with such confusion that the story was hardly heard and the pictures were scribbled on rather than colored. At the time for worship, each child introduced himself to her and the lead teacher told her what the "Daddy did for a living." When she came to one child, she said, "Oh, Sharon doesn't have a Daddy. God took him away to heaven after his car crashed." "He's dead," Sharon said with certainty.

The superintendent, upon reporting the visit to the Christian education committee, recommended placing a warm, comforting older woman from a retirement home in the classroom to take care of attendance and to make phone calls to the absentees. The children talked to her and she listened. The satellite teachers talked to her and she listened.

It became more and more evident that there was one decision maker and that she was not liked so much as feared by the other teachers. As time went on she became uncomfortable and more defensive than before. Finally, she suggested that she resign and let the older lady take over. "Oh, no," the golden-ager cheered. "I'm doing exactly what I want to and no more. Why not have Enid head our group next year? Pass the hard jobs around, Alice."

With that Enid was appointed, informally. The former decision maker stepped down and before long stepped out completely. At that point, the general superintendent swept in with her list of goals and the curriculum materials corresponding to what the rest of the school was using.

"Christ is better represented," she told the teachers at their appreciation dinner, "through all of us acting on the conviction that we are, children and adults alike, salt of the earth; rather than through some of us assuming that we are set on earth to pound in the crystallized sayings of Christ."

SETTING YOUR OWN GOALS

Your objectives and goals are pretty much your own congregational and denominational business, depending upon your form of government. Three objectives for every person responsible for setting educational goals in

64

the congregation are: (1) to see the teachers at work, (2) to ask and to listen to the person before reporting disapproval, and (3) to be familiar with the curriculum materials used.

1. *Seeing the teachers at work* for the first time is a revelation of hope or despair. A minister who was firmly in support of the church school, if it took itself seriously, had scheduled services of worship concurrent with the church school. He saw the children often enough, because they were frequent worshipers. He had not, however, been to classes. One Sunday a ministerial candidate was occupying the pulpit, and the pastor had an opportunity to visit. He was enthused and then ecstatic. "They were all learning," he told the elders, "and even the teachers were having fun." A four-year-old girl who had been in the service of worship each week since the age of six weeks had looked him over and said, "I didn't know you, God, without your dress." The adults laughed, explained the joke, and introduced the pastor once more.

2. *Asking and listening before reporting disapproval* can save you embarrassment. There are reasons for the choice of techniques, methods, and order of events in a well-run class. There may be reasons in a poorly taught class, too, and those you might well report.

An elder visited a class of fourth-graders during a time when they were preparing a Christmas marionette show —all except one boy. He walked around singing and slapping people on the back. The teacher did nothing until time for the show to premiere. "Bobby," she said firmly as she put her arm on his shoulder, "sit down and stop singing. It's time for the show."

The elder asked her why the boy was allowed to be unruly. The teacher explained that when everyone else was making a lot of noise, it was all right. The elder disagreed. "But they were working," he insisted.

"Bobby is severely retarded, Mr. Spencer," the teacher told him. "He's home for Christmas vacation, and we want him to feel welcome here."

When there is no such reason for like behavior, you should report disapproval of the condition. Perhaps the teacher needs a partner or help on how to maintain order.

3. *Being familiar with the goals of the curriculum materials used* is a fairly simple matter. Every curriculum series has a prospectus or a position paper that explains the scheme, delineates goals, and presents a sketch of the subject matter. Materials vary greatly. Some begin and end with a study of the Scriptures. Some begin with life situations and bring the Scriptures to bear on them. Others run it the opposite way. You may well criticize the materials, but reserve your judgment of the teacher until you know whether he and not the materials are at fault, in your estimation.

No one expects you to read every book, guide, manual, and magazine. Reading curriculum materials all the way through is akin to no afternoon recess when you're in third grade. Reading only parts at random does you little good and sometimes misinforms you from the generalizations you are bound to draw. After you read the position paper, get the help of someone who knows the whole story. Person to person beats person to paper.

You are not reading so that you will approve of whatever is done. You are gaining background for a situation in which you are placed as judge. You well may find out that the materials need changing. You can't build a case, then, without reading further.

IN CONCLUSION

Educational goals change because circumstances and congregations change. With experience we learn more about learners and teachers. We get wiser about what

66

can be accomplished and what cannot. We get better at writing educational goals. Don't have them engraved. Write them on sheets of newsprint with a grease pencil. Look them over each year with the cold eye of experience, and change what no longer is appropriate.

Get accustomed to change. When we become too fond of our innovations to give them up, we become exactly like the people who presented us with knotty problems when we first began upsetting old routines.

cleaning
the house
for action

Now that you and your co-workers have begun to think about what you want to accomplish and how you're going to do it, look over your structure, time schedule, use of space, and use of leadership for the time reserved for teaching. Review the schedule, content, and intention of your plans for teacher and leader education.

In all probability much of what structure you have can stay the same for the time being. Unless one of your objectives is to expand the time given to church school and change the day of the week, these things aren't likely to be different. There is a misconception abroad that a change in structure or schedule is a surefire improvement. It well may be, if it's done at the right time—*after* a fairly long period of effective teacher education. Otherwise the teachers will continue as they always have, only at a different time or in a different organizational box. Wednesday instead of Sunday for church school does not ensure you against poor education. Indeed, there have been places where changing the day allowed the teachers twice as much time for doing as shabby a job as they had on Sundays.

No, the key to a clean house for education in the faith is well-informed leadership both in and around the classroom. The structure and schedule, then, will arise from the group and serve teachers and pupils. It is perilously easy to let organization be our master and to forget to reappraise its place and functions occasionally.

WE'VE ALWAYS DONE IT THAT WAY

In a small church in the mountains, corporate worship was held in the sanctuary and the whole church school met in an adjoining hall. There was no basement and no other rooms. The tradition was to have the services and the school simultaneously. At one time there was a grain of sense in the plan. People came on horseback and in wagons. It was late in the morning by the time they got there and near evening by the time some got home. Nowadays they come in pickup trucks and cars, but for years after the advent of the automobile, the practice continued. Why? *"Because we've always done it that way."*

The classroom procedures were chosen in deference to the worshiping community. The pupils did not sing. It would disturb the adults. They met at round tables all over the room and a teacher told stories while the young children colored pictures hectographed by the superintendent, and having only a casual relationship with what was being told. Teachers of older children worked on Bible study with them, but the boys and girls were encouraged to be as silent as they could and to use the quietest voices they could when called on to speak.

It's true, they did not bother the adults. But the three congregational hymns, the piano, and every word uttered by the minister came into the well-contained classroom.

When a new minister came a few years ago, he told the men and women while he was being interviewed by the pulpit committee that the tradition had to be discontinued if he were to come. There wasn't much feeling in favor of continuing as they had, and the decision to change was the beginning of new emphases in the church—adult education and teacher-leader education.

Significantly, when an area master teacher demonstrated small-group, team, and individual working techniques with sixth-graders, the children whispered to her. She said: "I like soft voices, because my own sounds better soft. But whispers are for secrets. We're working on The Gospel According to Matthew—the good news of Jesus Christ. *Talk* about it."

The adults had short-term courses and one continuing class. For the first time in the memory of any member, men taught church school. And for the first time, children went to church with their families. The singing in both church and church school sounded lusty because of the combination of children's and adults' voices. The minister had a fine singing voice and on occasion taught the congregation a new hymn between church school and corporate worship.

One of the women, commenting on the changes in people within the congregation, said, "It's a magnificent feeling to live in the golden age of one's church, and to know it."

YOUR OWN SITUATION

You may feel as a new administrative officer that many changes are called for right at the moment. Sometimes, in order that education goes on, you have to move fast.

70

Some classes may be too large for the rooms in which they're housed. Grouping by traditional grading or the first letter of the last name may result in an overbalance of boys to girls or vice versa. A self-starting, independent working group of children may be assigned to a tool and die maker of a teacher who has his work cut out for *them*. A shrinking violet or a Wagnerian opera star may need a co-teacher to improve the chemistry in the classroom. And some teachers may seem totally unprepared for their jobs session after session.

We'll deal with all these problems, because they are important if not crucial to an effective church school. Another factor is as crucial, however: the *way* in which change is accomplished. There is no rule that could apply to all educational systems in churches, except to say that to live in a situation for a while should help you to establish what changes can, should, or must come first. Make a list of changes during your first year in the job, and arrange and rearrange the items in the order in which they should be tackled. If you take time, you will develop tactics and strategies reflecting a wisdom you didn't know you had and a sense of proportion for which you'll be forever grateful.

Turning a time and place set aside for learning into a time and place where learning happens takes more than a housecleaning or a strong personality in charge. It takes men of vision leading the willing blind, the patient listening to the intolerant, the placid soothing the cantankerous, and all reasoning together.

LIKELY PROBLEMS WITH PEOPLE

Here are some of the problems you might run into your first year and ways in which others solved them or prevented the situation from getting worse.

"There are three elderly ladies in one big room and twenty-five three-year-olds in another." In three churches

this kind of problem was solved swiftly and easily. In one it was not. In the first of the three churches the women were told what the problem was and *they* suggested they remove their piano, easy chairs, floor lamps, and a couple of small rugs a deceased member of the dwindling group had made for them. The large carpet remained for the three-year-olds. "The church bought that anyway, girls," the teacher reminded them. They moved from their large living room to one that fit them better. In the second and third churches there were no available rooms on the first floor, and some of the members couldn't function on stairways. In the one church a ramp was built from a back door to a room in the basement. In the other the parsonage living room suited the class well.

Most older people are not vindictive. They just don't like to move. They develop a sense of ownership of their classroom and may forget that it, along with all the other rooms, belongs to the church. Though you won't endear yourself for insisting on the principle of church property, you will never regret making it a known policy.

In the church where a women's class would not move, the wife of the pastor emeritus was the teacher. The present minister advised that she be allowed to use the room, since the couple would, within the year, go to a retirement home in another city. When she left, the group decided, apart from any consideration of the use of the room, to meet weekdays in one another's homes. The problem was solved only by circumstances. Here, not enforcing the policy of the church property was probably politic and certainly considerate.

"I have thirteen boys and two girls in fourth grade. The girls won't come." Churches have solved this one in a number of ways, and though a few diehards still doubt the wisdom of the solutions, there are administrators and teachers abounding who know that one idea or another has worked for them.

72

There is nothing sacred about having a fourth-grade class. If your materials are for third- and fourth-graders, combine forces and mix the age groups. The fourth-graders may be able to read better than the third-graders, and can be most helpful in small-group work. If you have closely graded materials, decide which you're going to use and here again work with the third-graders. With three-year cycle curriculum materials fourth- and fifth-graders work well together with the fourth-graders sometimes needing help, but generally keeping up rather well.

There is nothing sacred, either, about coeducational classes. You might have a boys class if you don't become so enamored of the idea that you keep having one when you don't need it. Some teachers complain that boys as a group are hard to handle. Others don't say that at all. Give the boys to someone who likes to teach them.

"There aren't enough in any grade for a class." Here is an opportunity for a broadly graded class. It can be simple or very sophisticated in design. It most closely resembles the organization of a one-room school.

In a simple setup, where fewer than fifteen first- through sixth-graders worked with two teachers, the materials used were for first- and second-graders. Older children read to the younger ones and they all did a number of different art projects. At the end of two years the group was split. The third- and fourth- and fifth-graders used the materials for third and fourth grades. The first- and second-graders had one teacher and used their own materials. One of the women, who keeps her finger on the pulse of the groups, thinks the necessary adaptations have improved the teaching and increased pupil interest.

In a more sophisticated setup with a professional, seasoned teacher, eight boys and girls from first through seventh grades worked individually and in small groups on materials and projects suitable for their own age level.

73

They had conferences with the teacher about their work. It was a busy group where the boys and girls were free and informal with one another but intent on getting work done. Each child of third grade and above kept a record of his assignments. All boys and girls gathered for singing, and performed ably with the accompaniment of a guitar and more often *a cappella*.

Sometimes broadly graded classes can be useful for a couple of years, and if the problem of too few in an age group changes, return to your conventional system. You needn't make decisions for posterity. You make them for the time being.

"That is a terrible combination of students." Those combinations come along, and you have to try to do something about the group behavior. An observer in the classroom can generally figure out who the ringleaders are. They can be separated and put in different classes. Again we say, they needn't be in a class because their names begin A-H, because they are of one or the other sex, or in a particular grade. Think about who they *are* and who the teachers are. Don't dwell on factors they can't do much about.

In one sixth-grade class there were identical twin boys who were exceedingly mischievous. They were put in separate classes. It was only after the director of children's work secretly placed a name tag on each one's back that it was discovered that they started out in one class, left for a drink of water, and switched. Why? Just for fun.

One time in that same church, there were at least twelve girls in fifth grade whom the teachers branded the mafia. They were placed, a few in each class. They were given teachers who knew what they were in for and were prepared. They were devoted to disturbing the peace in whatever way they could. There were three in one class who became stagestruck and put on a play for all elementary-age children. It was the only time all year that the other

74

nine were interested in what was going on. Fortunately, they were not incorrigible the next year—almost, but nowhere near to the degree of the previous year. It is worthy of report to note that every girl came from a home with a mother and father who were either nominal church members or unaffiliated. One mother said: "If you don't want Carol there, I'll keep her at home. But she's a pest here too." A harried lawyer fresh from the juvenile court room, said, "Can't the church *enforce* some standards of behavior?" It can, but it's a good bit easier if the home does too.

Sometimes a class that is together by virtue of age group zips right through the church school, mystifying the best teachers. They are generally not interested in learning, and upon checking with the day school, one finds the same thing true there. Sometimes in regrouping, discipline improves. But it may get worse throughout the school instead. You may have to keep them together and not expect much from them.

One teacher discovered that in her group of renegades she had a cartoon artist and a guitar player. The group was in the sophomore class by this time. She asked if they'd like to entertain the group in some way. Surprised at the offer, they worked up a skit that she said was worthy of TV, *after all children were in bed.* The artist's running comments as he drew faces of the minister, the chief of police, the high school principal, and the girl who had won the Citizenship Award would have given a psychiatrist a good week's work.

"The teacher and the group just don't get along." That can happen. Classroom chemistry is a mystery. Sometimes the addition of another teacher in the room helps. Other times, it becomes evident that the teacher and some of the pupils don't *like* one another. Adults are quite capable of prejudiced thinking. They might not like long hair, gum-chewing, steel-rimmed glasses, gig-

gling girls, Italians, rich kids, or doctors' children. No child need go through a church school not being liked. Remove the teacher to another group. Take the offensive personalities to another group. Give the second teacher responsibility for those receiving the brunt of the prejudice. But do something to alleviate the situation. Tell the teacher why you're transferring him or the students. Most of the time you'll hear justification for the action ending like this: "Well, that's just the way I am. He'll have to get used to meeting people like me. Adults don't change." Well, they can. And, in the church, they should at least try.

Don't give up on teacher or pupils in a mismatching. If the teacher knows why you are rearranging classes, he may eventually decide not to teach. He may go away in a huff, either permanently or temporarily. If you keep calm and *friendly,* he probably will too. These people need listeners too. Be one.

"He's an inadequate teacher. He just can't do it." You might give a person like this one a capable partner or see if he can teach in a group. Find out what he can do well, and let him do that. The age group may be wrong for him.

In a Midwestern church a man who used to teach senior highs works now with two-year-olds. They don't make him nervous, he says. Indeed they don't. They crowd around him as if he were Santa Claus. In the same church a social group worker tried her person-to-person approach with a fifth- and sixth-grade class of girls. It was disaster to the end, which fortunately came quickly. She was asked to be the teacher of a group of young couples who said she did an excellent job. So did she. "If I know when I fail, I must know when I succeed," she commented.

Inadequate teachers aren't the problem teachers, really. They generally find their niche with your help or quit.

"That new teacher is lost. I didn't have time to do much helping." When teachers come in to replace someone in the middle of the year, you need to give them plenty of moral support and even pitch in and help, if they need you. You may find an experienced substitute who will help the person for two or three sessions, even to showing him how the experienced teacher plans a session. Team teaching supports the newcomer and educates him in many ways. If you can't arrange a permanent team, try the substitute partner until the new one has his feet on the ground.

One remarkable woman in a small church in the northeast does nothing else for the Christian education program but teach a few Sundays with a new teacher in any age group. Few churches are so blessed to find that capacity in one person. Most can find a few individuals who might agree to offer that kind of help.

"The substitutes are terrible this year." If they are, they need the same kind of help the incoming teacher does. It is hard enough to come in on a regular basis if you are inexperienced. Think how much harder it is to get a different group each time or not work more than once in six weeks.

You will always have substitutes who know what they're doing if they plan with the regular teachers and know ahead of time what is expected. You probably will never have enough of that kind. With team teaching and co-teaching the school is not so crippled when a teacher does not come for a Sunday or two. It is an excellent idea to get a substitute-partner, so that substitutes learn a little about how to be a helper.

"We have to get rid of that teacher." There are some do's and don'ts. The don'ts first.

1. Don't put everyone on a two-year contract with an enforced sabbatical just to get one person out. Some peo-

ple like to teach, miss being teachers, and should teach all the time. It's not an everyday occupation, it's only once a week. It's lack of courage and honesty along with the fear that we lack the tact that propels us into schemes that do us educational harm in the long run. We go to such great effort to ease out a teacher who should not be on our faculty, and exert so little energy, usually, to make the life of a good teacher more pleasant.

2. Don't be unkind. We work in a church and teach children that kindness is our way. And it is if we take our teaching seriously. Aims and objectives were crowding out one teacher who demanded a hearing with the session of a Presbyterian church. She came and presented her complaints. The elders listened and asked her questions about why she was opposed to the present system. She had feeble answers at best and was ill at ease. Finally one of the elders said: "Georgia, why don't you quit? You've worked so hard for so long. It's time you rested on your laurels. If you're not getting along, quit while you're ahead." Georgia did, and no hard feelings.

Now the do's.

1. Try to change as much as you can in the classroom. One teacher who was old and dearly loved by both fellow teachers and pupils was not using any curriculum materials. She had no scheme of instruction. She came and worked the pupils out in the same way each Sunday. Once she told them stories, and then she forgot to do that. Gradually, teachers were added to her staff and she became known as superintendent. The group was divided and she played the piano for both groups, enriching both by her vibrant personality. The teachers followed curriculum materials available from the church. In her last days she forgot whether or not she had been to each group. But she stayed in the church school, because it meant so very much to her. She was simply not instrumental any

longer. One day she went home from church, had a heart attack, and died. The newspaper reported her age as seventy-six and stated that she had taught church school for sixty years.

2. Show your appreciation. A man who had taught seventh-graders for almost ten years with an iron hand in an iron glove became particularly abusive one year. The young people complained that he was unreasonable, and not much was done about looking into his class. One day a boy came to the church office for a Band-Aid for a cut that obviously needed stitches. The man had struck him with the scissors. The teacher was confronted during the week by two Christian education committee members. He admitted cutting the boy and said that young people were increasingly hard to handle. One of the committee members asked, "Have you thought of resigning?" The man had many times, but he knew teachers were hard to get. He was told that anytime he wanted to resign, he could. "If you teach for one year," one of the men told him, "we appreciate you and know you love the church. You have taught for almost ten. You can serve the church elsewhere now."

3. Be honest. This rule matches "Don't be unkind." Being honest does not mean unveiling the unvarnished truth all at once. No one wants to hear that. It means not telling lies.

IN CONCLUSION

Much of what you do and how you do it depends on the disposition of the church. Think big. And think big in the way the congregation does.

Individualized and small informal group teacher education of forty teachers may be regarded as big to one person and as if nothing is happening to someone else.

Some men and women must know that the lights are on in the church building every night in order to be convinced that people are learning something. When two or three teachers sit in a living room and plan a session or a unit in the name of Christ, he is there. We all know the church is not the rocks, wood, and roofing of the building. But we forget it.

Working interdenominationally may be effective in numbers in an area and not in content. The reverse may be true somewhere else. At a morning neighborhood coffee party a woman noted that precisely because there were present a Jew, two Roman Catholics, three Methodists, a Zen Buddhist, and a Unitarian, the subject talked about most was religion. "I never heard so much about other faiths in any other place," confessed one of the Methodists.

Whatever you do to change things so that you have a more effective school, you will find that you are learning a great deal yourself. Always remember, you're not killing snakes; you are helping to change people. It takes time and quiet, gracious persistence.

school is in session

If you and your co-workers have planned together effectively for realistic eventualities, you may well be accused of doing nothing the first day you are there while church school is in session. This is a tribute to efficiency, not a criticism.

In a fairly large suburban church it was the custom to register every child each fall on the first Sunday after Labor Day. The Christian education committee, a parents committee, and the official board members all sat before shoe boxes of 5″ × 7″ registration cards with two tissue carbon copies of the form attached. It was an unqualified big deal. But the records were clean each year—for that Sunday.

The children and young people went to their departments, where, because no one was sure who was coming, there were no class lists. There wasn't a whole lot of time for class anyway after standing in line. Teachers of younger children accepted those who came bearing their carbon copies of the registration forms. They tried to do no more than welcome those who came and relieve any anxiety or fatigue caused by standing in line. Older children gathered in a large room grouped by grades. The superintendent counted off 1-2-3-4 and sent all those of one number to a classroom. Young people swarmed to the chapel, where they were told to come back the next week and to leave their carbon copies in the offering plates with their money.

The adults who brought their children straggled into corporate worship as late as the hymn after the sermon. The minister said he felt as if he were preaching in a cafeteria.

One year the parents committee adjourned to the church kitchen for coffee in between church school sessions. A woman sighed, "There *must* be a better way!" And at that moment efficiency was born.

The group realized that with the exception of twenty or thirty children and young people, the registrants had been there last year. One of the men remarked that the year he taught eighth-graders his class book looked like a date book by Christmas. Only the ones who registered on the Sunday after Labor Day were alphabetized and entered in the books. The others were penciled in by the teacher when they arrived, mostly without addresses, phone numbers, or parents' names. The next year, the parents vowed, would be different. It was.

During the summer all the last year's registrants were checked for frequency of attendance. Where no address was entered in a class book, the teacher was called and asked if the name was unknown to the committee. If a pupil had not been present for a prolonged period, someone called his home. (Most of these people had moved. Some were going to other churches.)

Class lists were made up and given to the teachers with the information that more registrants were likely to appear. The lists were assembled on the basis of attendance so that in every class there was a balance of frequent and sporadic attenders. Permanent roll books were not made up until late in October.

The first Sunday after Labor Day came. The Christian education committee arrived on the scene along with the hardworking parents committee. Registration tables were set up with the shoe boxes, 5″ × 7″ cards and carbon copies of them. Twenty-eight people were registered. School began in earnest that Sunday. New registrants were welcomed and initiated in a way proper for strangers within the gates of Christendom. They were noticed.

The Christian education committee members made the rounds of the departments and, the minister reported, were the only ones late for worship. The parents committee, at coffee in the kitchen, agreed that it was not a hard job. It was an easy job, done leisurely, carefully, and at the right time.

AFTER THE FIRST DAY

Your job is *not* to stay in the halls and talk to other administrators. If things go smoothly, you'll have plenty of time for that after your work is done. Decide among you who will support whom on the staff. At first, check in before the session begins. Talk with the pupils in the class. Ask the teachers if you can help in any way. After a few weeks, drop in and don't ask. By then they'll know you will help if they need something.

Observe a whole session and note the responses of the students to the teachers, the relationship between class members, and their reaction to the content of the study.

Ask questions of the teachers about aspects of the session you didn't understand. If a teacher asks for help that you cannot give, tell him of someone who might be able to help. *Never* send someone to a teacher without warning. If he knows you are aware of his problems in class, he is not as likely to be defensive when you offer someone's assistance. Sending someone unheralded is a little like calling your doctor for your neighbor who looks sick.

If more than one teacher needs the same kind of help and acknowledges it, ask someone to counsel with them at an agreed-upon meeting time. It needn't be a meeting with an open invitation, although it could be. The offer of help should be made to "anyone who needs help in . . . ," not "all teachers." The only time *all* teachers really need to be under one roof at one time is during church school sessions.

WHOM YOU MIGHT ASK TO HELP

Before you ask anyone to help a teacher, define the problem in your own mind. If it is a classroom problem, ask someone with experience in the classroom. That may sound like an all too obvious conclusion; but there is a misconception in the land that men and women in bureaucratic positions must know all the answers or they wouldn't occupy a drawer in the bureau. Of course, this is an erroneous idea. Many of the functions performed by bureaucrats make the life of a classroom teacher easier. They write and edit curriculum materials; they design leadership education courses. They are sometimes specialists in the teaching of one age group. They are not paragons of education or the epitome of the well-organized D.C.E. or pastor. They are frail human beings with a job to do just like the rest of us.

If there isn't a veteran teacher in your church that you feel could work on special problems, there may be one

84

in a church nearby. Your area Christian education consultant might be able to name someone who uses the same curriculum materials your church does and who has taught the same age group as the teachers seeking help.

PROBLEMS YOU MIGHT EXPECT

Listing problems may sound like a depressing occupation. In reality, it prepares us for some of the on-the-spot counseling we need to do, and it encourages us to plan ahead in our search for specialists.

Keeping order is almost always a problem somewhere in the church. Although observing the class gives many clues in solving discipline problems, there are unthreatening, fairly impersonal ways to help teachers.

In a panel discussion one evening three day school teachers discussed the importance of a good climate in the classroom, and answered many questions afterward. One was a high school teacher in the suburbs; another was a teacher of junior highs in a black ghetto neighborhood; the third taught elementary music in a private school. They agreed at several significant points. One was that their goal was self-discipline, not merely arbitrary law enforcement. Another was that older boys and girls know you can't force them to act in one way. A third was that students learn because they want to, or they simply occupy a space. The teacher from the ghetto school said that he never told a seventh- or eighth-grader, "You must not do that." He always said instead, "The rule in this room is that if you throw a pencil, you go and pick it up." The authority was placed in the rule, and not in the person of the teacher.

In answering questions afterward, the music teacher told of her use of games in promoting good relationships among the students. One of the church school teachers asked why she wanted the children to get along together;

she supposed it would be easier to teach if they were quiet. The teacher answered, "Singing, thinking, and learning are better done in concert than in isolation booths." This prompted the high school teacher to say that many of our efforts to keep cold order instead of a warm learning climate stem from our fear of the pupils.

Other panels as useful as the one described might include master teachers from the area or your own experienced teachers who have arrived at healthful classroom climates. If they are at all articulate, they generally know what stages they went through to get where they are now. Your aim is to get people with whom the teachers feel comfortable, so that they will ask questions and get straight, realistic responses.

Getting things done in an hour is sometimes a difficulty with teachers of kindergarten through second grade. There are so many skills the children still have not mastered that the teachers find themselves involved in time-consuming activities that not always are too valuable to the children. If this situation prevails, a meeting is probably *not* the most effective means of attacking the issue. Observation, conversation, and planning together are far more helpful.

The teachers learn through planning with an experienced or professional educator to choose those activities which children can do themselves and to enlist parents to help out. They also learn to move from one segment of the hour to another smoothly, to sense the disposition of the group, and to offer short change-of-pace activities. Many church school teachers of these age levels have learned such things after years of wasting time at little tables with little people unable to color little things in order to cut them out with little scissors.

An hour isn't very long if it's planned well. Two hours is far better if they're planned well. But an hour is long enough to do a creditable job.

"We're bored" was the complaint of the senior highs, and they rested the blame on the teacher. He wasn't what you'd call a bundle of jokes; he was more of a variations-on-one-theme man. The minister of education, who was a former prep school English teacher, convinced the man to allow the young people to teach themselves. They worked in small groups and individually, preparing sessions much as a group of teachers would. The man became an enthusiast for the method and has lately been visited by other senior high teachers who value the opportunity to observe the class in action. One day during his session he was drinking coffee in the church kitchen when one of his students came in. "One of those teachers is visiting us, and wants to meet you." The others laughed. "Get up there and teach, Gary! Somebody wants to watch you!"

Teaching adults presents entirely different problems. They aren't overtly rude or disorderly. Neither are they usually as eager to learn new things and struggle with ideas in the way high school students are. Two young adults from a small church attended a weekend workshop for discussion leaders called EQUIP. They learned how to ask questions in order to get others involved with the content of the discussion. They practiced techniques in listening to the responses so that they could pose more questions on an even deeper level of thought. Enthused, they returned and virtually turned the adult class upside down with excitement and formed another discussion group which meets in the homes of participants.

All area meetings are not as valuable as this one was. It came at the right time in the life of that church and in the lives of the two women. It had a specific, announced goal and was organized to achieve it.

Planning a unit is new to many teachers who have taught a long time. Recent educational materials for children, youth, and adults are organized around concepts or ideas.

Though many suggestions are given for the order of events and directions are included for projects, the planning of the sessions is ultimately up to the teachers. It always was, but with a session plan in front of them, it looked as if the job was already done. Teachers of units can no longer pretend to teach a class by reading the "lesson" on the way to church at the stoplights. The whole unit has to be read and the choice of what segments are taught at what time is best made in the company of at least one other teacher. Most teachers who have worked with units such as these for a year or more have found their whole teaching experience has improved. Just as tailor-made clothes fit better than the mass-produced ones, so do custom-made session plans.

The symptoms of a problem with unit-planning vary. Occasionally, they take the form of criticisms of the materials. Most often an observer can notice a lack of variety in the session, no apparent relationship between the parts of the session, and little use of resources outside of the teacher's guide or pupil's book.

One teacher confessed in November that she was still on Unit 2 in a study of Moses, while everyone else was on Unit 4. Upon visiting the class, the coordinator found that the entire group was working on one page in the pupil's book, and did so for the entire session. She suggested small group and independent work as described in the teacher's guide.

There are films and filmstrips on unit-planning. Teacher's guides attempt to explain ways to do it, but when you come right down to one class, one set of teachers, and one particular church, every group has to decide on its goals and work toward them in their own ways, with the resources as part of their support system. The children and young people can have a part in the planning too.

These issues or problems you might expect are not unhealthy in a church. They keep you and the teachers thinking and acting together in order to improve the situation. It is the next kind of problem that demands your wits at the moment something happens.

THE UNEXPECTED

Some of the best and worst things have happened at church because they were surprises.

"Of course he's welcome, but . . ." came to a teacher's lips when a fourteen-year-old deaf boy came to his eighth-grade class. The boy was in a foster home for weekends and had only recently gone to a resident school for the deaf. He was not retarded, but uneducated even about his own handicap. He made strange noises and made clumsy overtures of friendship to the other young people.

The superintendent heard the man talking with the foster parents, joined them, and said heartily: "We're glad to see Leo. I'll show him around the church so he'll feel at home." The teacher was relieved, because he had not the slightest notion of how to work with the boy. Leo was not a regular attender, but as his time at school increased, his ability to be in a group of hearing people without disturbing anyone grew noticeably. His foster mother wrote a letter of appreciation to the teacher at the end of the year. "We don't know what he gets out of it," she wrote. "But lately he's forced us to come more often, because he likes being there."

Children and young people with handicaps can fit into most groups unless they cannot tolerate the presence of other people or have been the victims of poor training. It may be necessary to assign one person to a severely re-tarded child who is unable to maintain the attention span of the group. Walking around with him may be a diverting pleasure for him. It behooves us to find out as much as we can about the specific handicap and the expectations of school and parents for him. It is tragic enough that we sometimes "spoil" our gifted students.

How much worse it is if we do that disfavor to one whose row is hard enough to hoe with the best education.

"Miss Olson's in there cryin'," a six-year-old girl told the director of Christian education. The director went in to find out what had gone wrong. Everything. Miss Olson told a long, tearful story about the children not liking her as much as she liked them, of her roommate not liking her, of a man who didn't marry her twenty-two years ago, and of her uncaring sister in Chicago.

The director listened, waited until Miss Olson had swabbed the deck, and walked with her to her apartment. The minister called in the afternoon, and Miss Olson went into therapy the following week.

Sometimes we can see danger signals as a person teaches or talks with us, but most of us aren't trained to pinpoint them. Of one thing you can be sure. When a person is as disturbed as Miss Olson was, it is *not* just the class, the other teachers, or a chance remark from someone in the hall that causes the disturbance. *Don't take the blame,* even if you did happen to tell a story about an old maid in front of someone like her. All that happened, unfortunately, to Miss Olson on that Sunday morning was that the inattention of the children during the telling of a story added one more rock to her sack that was almost past carrying as it was.

"The ceiling fell in!" shouted a young woman as she shepherded fifteen children and a shaken partner from the old house used for first- and second-graders. She was assured by the minister who told her crisply that the carelessness of men and the providence of God had worked together to make the house unusable.

She had kept calmer than her partner and quickly took the children outside where she examined them for surface cuts and shook plaster out of their hair. Then as an afterthought she said: "Well, you look like a pretty spiffy bunch. I think we should all go to church." They entered the sanctuary as the minister said "Amen" to his sermon, stood for the final hymn and benediction, and went home.

The house was torn down, and a neighbor who was not a member of the church offered his basement recreation room to the first- and second-graders. He told them that the floor was cold, but that the ceiling was reliably glued to the floor above it.

"I can't find Billy!" a distraught woman cried after most of the people had left a reception following corporate worship. Everyone snapped into action. Being lost may or may not be a crisis. The director of Christian education stayed in the social hall so that the detectives could come back and report. The police were called and before some of the church searchers returned, the desk sergeant called back to say that one of the cruising cars had picked up the small child north of town as he meandered along a median strip between lanes of a busy highway. The mother was told Billy was all right and promptly fainted, came to, wept, and received her easygoing five-year-old. He said he had decided he'd had enough waiting, and had begun walking home.

When a child is lost, someone has to keep calm and act quickly. If the child is found and the parents are lost, he may be upset. Don't refer to *him* as lost. He knows exactly where he is. He is looking for the folks he came in with.

Some individuals find the behavior of the calm person infuriating. They assume it means that the person doesn't care. Of course, it doesn't. It is quite probable that the old pro who can keep cool has had innumerable experiences involving what we call *non-crises*.

THE UNEXPECTED NON-CRISES

It's up to you to decide what is and what is not a crisis. Not everyone sees an event in the same perspective.

A woman and man who have worked for over ten years as coordinators of the part of the church school serving babies through sixth grade have volunteered the following list of non-crises. Most reports of them come on the phone during the week; some come in person after church school from children and parents.

The couple react calmly, seriously, and always with a word of hope or a suggestion.

1. *Lost:* One navy blue coat, size 4, almost new, brass buttons, red, white, and blue crest on sleeve. No name tag.

Found: Same, only frayed, dirty, and with a torn lining. No name tag.

Response: "Bring the coat back with you next week, if you don't hear from us beforehand. Look carefully at all the coats before you decide which is yours. There are eight or ten exactly like the one you describe. Put a name tag in yours when you get it back. It will be the only coat with one."

2. *Confiscated by teacher:* one transistor radio.

Response: "What was his reason for bringing it?" And after checking with the teacher: "Mr. Hanson gave it to Pastor Helmstrom for safekeeping. Either you or your son may get it from him."

3. *Found by parent:* Tempera paint on shirt sleeve.

Response: "Yes, we use paint on Sundays. The children wear men's shirts and plastic aprons to protect their clothing." And upon checking with the teacher: "Mrs. Graff says that Jamie didn't paint last Sunday. He may have rolled on the edge of a painting that was drying while they acted out life in the wilderness. . . . Well, yes, they could have been lying on the floor. Moses and the people slept on the ground, you know."

4. *Reported by breathless five-year-old:* Alice Andurian chased me out of the room with a black marking pen.

Response: "Where is she now?" And upon investigation Alice was found with a distraught mother surveying long black marks on her dress, legs, and arms, put there by aforementioned Breathless Five-Year-Old before Alice seized the pen.

One man's crisis is another man's non-crisis. We'll never agree on them completely. This list belongs to one couple. They keep calm, because they know they can see the problem through. The habit of serenity will serve them during a real crisis, when someone needs all the support everyone can give him.

the christian year and your year

All the time you are concerned with getting and orienting new teachers, living around and learning from the old ones, and setting up goals for all of them, the Christian year advances. Don't neglect it. It offers a time of festival when we all say thank you in chorus.

LENT, A FESTIVAL OF GIVING

The whole church family participates in Lenten offerings such as One Great Hour of Sharing and The Bishop's Fund. There are filmstrips and publicity posters available for getting the word around about the offerings. They aren't a time-consuming project for an administrator. On the other hand, neither are they as concrete a project as one of special need in your own community. You need both, because we all should get used to giving in the dark. The national offerings are intended for the unforeseen tragedies and emergencies in which people have to get on their feet in a hurry. They remind us of just who our neighbors are.

The special project in your own church may be an all-out effort to support a short-term missionary from your congregation, a family in another country known to a missionary, or an exchange student in a college or seminary. It is specific, and the people know to whom they are giving and why.

In a downtown church of declining membership and increasing work with children and young people of the deteriorating neighborhood, there was a traditional giving project. The whole church, through The Welfare Federation, adopted a family in the neighborhood as anonymous parents. The boys and girls in the church school were told about the family and also that they were to bring a secret present wrapped and tied. It was to be something they would like to have very much themselves.

When all of the gifts were in, the minister, the superintendent, and a deacon delivered them to the Federation offices where they were opened. What was there?

    kaleidoscope
    jump rope
    Snoopy autograph dog
    magnifying glass
    red felt-nib pen
    assorted seals and gold stars
    squirrel tail
    book, *The Trumpet of the Swan*
    box of colored chalk
    magic slate
    Parchesi
    Monopoly

ten eight-cent stamps and stationery
　　　marbles
And the minister noted: no mittens, no handkerchiefs, and no soap.

Young people and adults are more able to give money to a known need than are children. Until one knows what fifty cents will buy that a nickel will not, bringing money is not as significant as bringing a present he'd like for himself. At Christmas, many more people remember to give to those who have less than they have than they do at Lent, when the poor are still poor.

Sometimes an all-church project isn't successful. There is always a reason. It may have been organized poorly, not publicized sufficiently, or not too meaningful to those who are asked to give. Those are common reasons, and inherent in them are your remedies. Organize well, publicize thoroughly, and pick a project with meaning to the young as well as the old. There are less obvious reasons for out-and-out failure or ineffectual results of a project.

In a large church school accustomed to all-church giving projects several times a year, it was determined that during Lent money would be raised for musical instruments for a school in Africa. The project was publicized; money was put in several big drums when the children brought it. A few used instruments were collected, and the enthusiasm during the collection was fairly high.

Suddenly the project was over. No results were publicized. No letters were sent from the young children to the school receiving the instruments. No report was made to the Christian education committee. Only the committee chairman wondered aloud what had gone wrong. As for the others in so large an organization, they assumed "it" was all taken care of by professionals.

Unfortunately, the professionals were the stumbling block rather than the channel they were expected to be. One of the ministers had wanted to send recorders to the school instead of the band instruments they had requested. The committee had honored the school's wishes, which were also those of the D.C.E. The minister, still adamant, took the money collected by the youth and sent for a hundred plastic, inexpensive recorders of inferior tone quality. Without that money and whatever else the youth collected, the band instruments could not be purchased. Without unanimity in the church school, the official board would not open up the giving opportunity to others in the congregation. The project failed because the professionals failed those they were employed to lead. It was not just the minister's impulsive action that was to blame; it was an inability of the entire employed staff to communicate, compromise, and accept the ugly in one another. The congregation—children, young people, and adults—was the victim. When such unfortunate battles occur, it is essential that they not affect the givers' attitudes toward giving and toward those who need what we have. The minute a school has adopted a "Who cares?" or "What's the use?" attitude, it is recipients of the gift who suffer most.

PALM SUNDAY

In a neighborhood church where adults, young people, and children mixed and met so often in their daily lives that they knew one another well, participation in corporate worship was a matter of course. A new minister in the church, who was festival inclined, ordered palms for the elementary church school children as well as the traditional ones for youth and adults. The children counted Sundays until Palm Sunday, so excited they were to be included in the palm-giving. They learned the final hymn to be sung in corporate worship and, as the congregation stood, marched down the center aisle and sang with dignity as they waved the palms they had just been given. Ladies cried into their handkerchiefs, and men's tears dripped on their hymnals. After the benediction, an air of celebration filled the sanctuary. "A multitude keeping festival."

The five-year-olds in the same church had made their own palm branches out of strips of construction paper. When the parents came for them, they were sweeping them on either side of the wide path and shouting through the ceiling: "Hosanna! Hosanna! Hurray for Jesus!" One young father, who had been moved by the decorum of the elementary children at worship, had unapologetic tears in his eyes once more when he quipped, "You can almost smell the donkey!"

EASTER

Easter is the high point of the Christian year. Without it the good news would not be with us. It is a time for everyone in the church, with or without families, to celebrate together.

In one church it was customary for the three- and four-year-olds to tiptoe softly to the gallery and look down at the lily-bedecked chancel and the singing congregation. Before doing so, to assure their ability to walk quietly, a singing game was played in which they jumped, ran, walked, and tiptoed. During the jump routine, a college boy swept into the room and snarled, "What *are* you doing?" The pianist looked up and answered: "Hang around, we're teaching them how to tiptoe. Then we'll teach you how to smile."

The tolerance to necessary educational noise is a *learned* response. Even some very young ladies and gentlemen feel that children should be unseen and not heard from in the church. Festivals of the church are memorable, and we want the children to grow up remembering the church. They, too, should be privileged to shout alleluia! on the day of resurrection.

THE LORD'S DAY

One other festival of the resurrection is sometimes overlooked as a time for the whole church to celebrate together. It is corporate worship. Children and young people have to be taught *about* worship, lest they dismiss it forever as something they don't understand, don't like, or aren't entitled to. They needn't have a little Children's Corner in the service in which the minister talks only to them. What both children and young people want is intelligent participation as fellow worshipers.

One Sunday after the fifth- and sixth-graders had been in church for the full hour rather than until just before the sermon, a sixth-grade girl said to her parents, "Good sermon today."

"What was it about?" her father asked.

"You were there. Don't you remember?"

"Well, yes, sort of. I just wondered if you did."

"Of course," she answered. "We take *notes*." She had recorded the text, the three points of the sermon, and summary.

Younger children have a hard time sitting for an hour. Some do very well at it with their parents, having done so since infancy. In a class, they can hardly be expected to stay immobile for so long a time when they cannot read and cannot understand the words of the Scripture, the sermon, or the hymns. Watching Baptism and witnessing the ordination of a child's father as an elder or a deacon are probably the kinds of services that would mean the most to five- through seven-year-olds. When children begin to study the Lord's Supper, they should witness the Eucharist even though the particular church may not invite them to participate until they are older.

Worship does not have to be child-centered to be significant to a child. There are times when a child is invited into the world of adults before he is initiated. Family tragedy is one and corporate worship is another. Children need firm, sympathetic support in addition to the assurance that you know they are children and they can trust you as grown-up human beings.

CHRISTMAS

There are grinches in the church who say that the sequenced study should not be interrupted for special holidays, as they call them. If Jacob hasn't made it to Egypt to be reunited with Joseph, he does so even if it's Sunday, December 25. Grinches are that way. One stole Christmas, remember.

If there are other opportunities to meet outside of the study hour, there is nothing unwholesome about getting Jacob into Egypt to see his son for Christmas. You can celebrate the festival of the birth of Christ at some other time.

When your time is limited to Sunday mornings, you may want to stop what you're studying and celebrate Advent. In most sequenced material you can find units to adapt to the season of Advent. In Biblical parlance, you are robbing Peter to pay Paul. You are using in December what was generally intended for February.

Older children and young people may be able to help you make the decision about what to study. They might want to get on with what they're doing or adopt a service to the local church community or far-flung mission of the church for the Advent season.

One sixth-grade class invited a class from another church to meet with them for six weeks to write and produce a Christmas puppet show which they presented many times. It was remarkably like *Amahl and the Night Visitors* for the story line, but the music, the lyrics, and the spoken word were all their own.

Pageants and whether or not to have them is a debatable question. The decision depends entirely on the pageant and the time you have to prepare for it. Increasingly, short

100

afternoon services of singing and simple tableaux are replacing the complicated, hard-to-hear three-scene pageant that ends just before Santa Claus rushes in to pass out oranges and jelly-filled candy.

Some churches have for many years held the same service each year. Costumes for the tableaux can be kept from year to year and look more appropriate though hardly more appealing than the assortment of flannel bathrobes used to. One rehearsal is all that is necessary for simple tableaux. The hymns and carols sung by the congregation can be learned throughout Advent in the church school. Choirs have regular times to rehearse throughout the year.

One such traditional service uses *The Christmas Story,* by Johannes Petzold, with the English adaptation by Theodore Klammer (Concordia Publishing House). It is a cantata designed for Christmas celebration in church, school, or home. Its simple nature makes it appealing to children, and the inclusion of small singing groups, instrumental music, solos, and congregational singing gives the work variety. The manger scene and the arrival of shepherds are the only necessary tableaux, although others could be added such as a prophet at the beginning and people in modern dress at the end.

What you do to celebrate Christmas in worship should reflect the church's attitude toward corporate worship. Where young children are present, as they should be in family services, you can expect things to happen that might not during a normal Sunday service of worship. In one church, during a Christmas vesper service, children of ten to twelve years old strode up the center aisle dressed in traditional festival costumes from all over the world. A few three- and four-year-olds wandered into the aisle to touch the costumes. One of the costumed girls took her sister's hand and led her to the manger in the chancel along with a few others who decided to come. It did not spoil the service; it enhanced it.

Instead of a pageant. Christmas came one year while a church in a rural village was being extensively repaired. The congregation was meeting in the town hall, where village and township board members met and smoked cigars. The building was in far worse condition than the church that was undergoing repairs, but it had a roof and a furnace.

The young people and youthful minister had been in accord since fall that Christmas would be a celebration at the town hall, so that everyone would know that Christ comes among us, steeple and chancel or not. The young people were not a cohesive group. They attended study groups with adults, assisted in the church school, and one girl made posters and banners for the district women's organization. There were many active young people, but, like adults in the church, they didn't know one another well. They attended five area high schools. The pastor was their clearinghouse.

He showed a committee of concerned young people several schemes for observing Christmas in the town hall. Only one hit their corporate fancy, and then with reservations. The minister had presented Louis F. Benson's poem "O Sing a Song of Bethlehem" for a show of great art on slides with Scripture read between stanzas. The senior highs said that the poem "sang," but none of that great art, whatever that was.

They agreed that turning the lights out and showing slides was an excellent way to keep from staring at the filthy, water-streaked walls with the crumbling plaster. But the slides were to be of today, because Jesus is. "And," added an articulate girl on the committee, "if he's not, forget him."

With the poem as a rough guide, a man and a senior high boy who were both amateur photographers set out to take pictures in the village and surrounding countryside. They began in October, not long after the church calendar meeting had been held to determine essential program for the year. When they brought their slides to the committee, the ones desired were set aside to be shown at the Christmas service. A woman was chosen to work in the church school with choral speaking selections from the Gospels, and the program was put together, hardly resembling the pastor's first attempt at a suggestion.

One of the hardest decisions to make, after it was determined that the whole service would be in darkness, was what tune should be used to sing the words of Louis Benson's poem. It is Common Meter Double, and there are many sturdy hymn tunes to that meter. However, "My Faith It Is an Oaken Staff" was a favorite hymn from church school days. When the young people discovered that the words *almost* fit the music, they altered only one line. It was not musically tasteless, and because everyone knew the tune well, it was a good choice for singing in the dark.

The church school children memorized the hymn and sang it to the accompaniment of a recorder played by a junior high girl. (The piano which had been moved from the church was dreadfully out of tune, because there was no heat in the town hall when it was not used and a bit too much when it was.) Words to the hymn for total congregational singing were put on slides. No rehearsal for the service involving every participant was necessary, because everyone was ready. As a consequence, a spontaneity pervaded the worship as it progressed.

This is how it went.

MINISTER: Isaiah 40:3-5
CHILDREN: O sing a song of Bethlehem,
    Of shepherds watching there,
And of the news that came to them
    From angels in the air:
The light that shone on Bethlehem
    Fills all the world today;
Of Jesus' birth and peace on earth
    The angels sing alway.

103

The slides shown quickly throughout the singing of the stanza were of farmers, farmland, dawn from a hill, sunset, an approaching thunderstorm, Holstein dairy cows, rolling hills, a baby strapped to his mother's back as she peers into a brooder house.

CHILDREN: O sing a song of Nazareth,
        Of sunny days of joy,
    O sing of fragrant flowers' breath,
        And of the sinless Boy:
    For now the flowers of Nazareth
        In every heart may grow;
    Now spreads the fame of His dear Name
        On all the winds that blow.

The slides were taken in the village. They showed folks chatting with the postmaster, children going to school, a softball game, a dog lying on Main Street, recess at the elementary school, two girls with bittersweet bouquets, a man standing in his chrysanthemum bed, a child lying in a gigantic pile of leaves, a priest in his cassock talking to several nuns, one with shoe roller skates slung over one shoulder of her habit.

CHILDREN: O sing a song of Galilee,
        Of lake and woods and hill,
    Of Him who walked upon the sea
        And bade its waves be still:
    For though, like waves on Galilee,
        Dark seas of trouble roll,
    When faith has heard the Master's word,
        Falls peace upon the soul.

The slides showed a group of young people and adults leaving a wooded area at a study center, a picnic at the lakeshore, sailboats, a rough lake with no boats, ice on the lake, ice fishermen with hand warmers, a woman at her window looking at the snow, people standing around after church, deacons and their wives washing Communion ware in the kitchen, the custodian dusting the Communion table.

CHILDREN: O sing a song of Calvary,
            Its glory and dismay;
        Of Him who hung upon the tree,
            And took our sins away:
        For He who died on Calvary
            Is risen from the grave,
        And Christ, our Lord, by heaven adored,
            Is mighty now to save.

The slides shown during the final stanza were of a funeral procession, a gravedigger, the village cemetery gate, the veterans memorial stone in the park, the cornerstone of the church, a memorial plate in a hymnal, the stained-glass window of the risen Christ with the symbolic representations of the Gospel writers surrounding him.

After the singing was over the seven small stained-glass windows at the side of the sanctuary were shown in sequence, each bearing a single symbol. They represented the birth, unknown life, baptism, ministry, crucifixion, resurrection, and Pentecost. The town hall was quiet.

Then to the accompaniment of the recorder and supported by the children's voices, the entire congregation sang the hymn as the words were projected on the wall.

Scripture was read in choral speaking, recorded on tape during church school sessions. The selections were:

Luke 2:1-14	Grades 1-4
Luke 23:44-49	Grades 5-6
Luke 24:44-48	Grades 7-8

John 21:25 was read by the minister in person, after which the children were given only their pitch and began

singing "Joy to the World." As the adults in the congregation joined them, the children left their seats, the lights were turned on, and quite informally the boys and girls joined their singing parents. Worship was over.

YOUR CHURCH YEAR

Aside from the ecclesiastical year, your own church has one. The latter schedule varies so widely from church to church, that in an Illinois town of 30,000, a committee of young people discovered seventeen different dates for observing Youth Sunday and even more than that number of congregations not observing it at all. In a Northwestern city of 10,000, there were four large, well-attended vacation church schools of two weeks' duration. In a city of almost 70,000 in the east, there was not one. In many areas of the country there are skeletal church schools in the summer. In whole regions, however, no church school is held after school is out. More and more, the beginning of the year is considered to be the Sunday after Labor Day rather than the old Rally Day of traditional Sunday school of the early twentieth century. It is the day folks come back, whether they've gone anywhere or not.

If you are dissatisfied with any part of the year as your church plans it, take a long look at what you don't like and think about how it could be better, or at the very least, different. The year divides itself quite naturally into the secular school year and summer. Even if you're dissatisfied with certain aspects of the school year, almost everyone is discontented about what is or is not done in the summer.

WHAT SHALL WE DO IN THE SUMMER?

Leadership is very often hard to get over the summer months. People plan to be gone off and on or go on the spur of the moment. Weekends lend themselves to camping trips and all-day outings. Sunday church school sessions, even when leaders have been found, are sometimes conspicuously short of pupils. Afternoon young people's gatherings, no matter how tailored to summer they may be, have often gone virtually unattended. The question becomes not so much, What *can* be done in the summer? but What *will people do* in the summer? More and more we have found that they are not enthusiastic about summer church school, daily vacation church school, and resident camps for the whole family or the children. Where it is still true that enthusiasm runs high, there isn't one good reason to change to another form. Your energies should go instead into making that form better.

No pattern no matter how old it is or who started it is sacred, nor should it be permanent. It is not the fault of the leaders and teachers that no one attends a very good program, if no one has come to find out what it's like. There may be too many diverting or necessary alternatives offered at the same time as vacation church school, church camp, and Sunday worship. Churches have experimented with new forms at new times, and it will not surprise you to find out that what works well in one place fails miserably in another. There is nothing but profit for you in examining the seeds that took root elsewhere. You know your own soil best.

Backyard play groups took the place of vacation church school for young elementary children in a sprawling suburban community. Five and six children gathered in their own neighborhood, sometimes in their own block to attend a well thought out program using the Cooperative Vacation Church School Series in most innovative ways. The neighborhood groups varied as to the degree of activity outside their backyards. Some groups took field trips and hikes, went on picnics and cookouts, and others stayed home to make butter, hear stories about what others were seeing, work on projects at a picnic table, and generally go and come at the appointed times.

All groups were broadly graded except one where there happened to be seven children in third and fourth grades in one neighborhood. The groups were called play groups, not work groups or vacation *school* of any kind. The emphasis was on playing together. Field trips became a form of play largely because the children looked upon them that way. In most groups the children were active planners with the teachers. It was not "What shall we do today?" at the beginning. Rather it was, "Tomorrow we can begin a nature mural, hike over to the duck pond, read about Uncle Ed again, or do you have another idea about how we could learn about the world around us?" The older children had many questions to answer through research. One group visited a forest products laboratory, another an observatory, and the third answered questions through the scientific method in the backyard where they met. Their experiments were written up in an agreed-upon form.

Neighborhood nursery schools for children of three and four have proved a boon to mothers even when the "schools" have been child care opportunities rather than educational ventures. One such gathering was made up of four children and two teen-agers who cared for the children five days a week from 9:00 to 11:00 A.M. They took the children to the park where they played, rested, and listened to stories as they wished. There was no set program and no goals except to get along well when the children chose to play together. The parents were charged a dollar a day, so that the girls would have enough money by the middle of August to go on a senior high work trip to the Southwest.

Neighborhood nursery schools are more a constructive way to use teen-agers' time than the children's. Mothers need to be certain the children will be well cared for before releasing them for so long a time.

Day camp, especially for city children, is an opportunity to learn to exist in the out-of-doors without having to do so for more than a day at a time. Going home every afternoon precludes homesickness and wilderness sickness. Boys and girls from the city find comfort in noise and are sometimes kept awake by the stark silence of the woods. One fifth-grade Chicago boy on an overnight put his watch outside his tent so that the ticking would not keep him awake. Another on the same trip asked, "What's that whooshing sound?" It was a slight breeze in the trees.

Campcraft is not the only area touched upon at day camp. Getting along and learning to like people person-to-person is something there is plenty of time to do. Working and playing two by two instead of in droves, pursuing a project in solitude, and learning to talk to and like an older person are privileges of day camping that inner-city life could but perhaps doesn't afford many children.

A fourth-grade girl summed up her day-camp experience at a park in Cleveland: "It was noisy and pushy on the bus. Then we got to the park and ran and ran. When we were tired, we sat down and I listened, and all around me I heard quiet, quiet, quiet. Then Jerri, our leader, helped us do what we wanted and never said mad things to us like, 'Hush up, hear?' or 'Forget you!' "

Day camp is not universally popular with fourth- through sixth-graders. When it was adopted as a substitute for a poorly attended vacation church school in a small southern Ohio town, it was received with little enthusiasm by the children. It was not that they already knew how to survive in the out-of-doors. There was much they didn't know even though the parks and natural wooded areas were near at hand. The teachers (not leaders) had chosen to bring the vacation church school curriculum materials outside. They weren't having day camp; it was the same old church school without the convenience of tables and chairs. The most popular activity of the whole summer was a trip to the art museum in Dayton. There were so many things about the city that the children didn't know that the following week they wrote to several ministers to find out what the possibilities were for learning more about Dayton. Just as we expand a city child's experiences by taking him to the country, so we should realize a small-town child's dream of learning about the city.

Go and see tours used to be the exclusive domain of affluent young people who wanted a vacation, a bus ride, and a look at another part of the country under the aegis of the church. With a little imagination it has taken many forms, all of which inform those who go of the work of the church with people.

Go and see tours can be family trips across the United States with home mission projects among the Indians being the work of the church to examine. In trips like that it is always courteous if not essential to write ahead so that someone is ready to show you around. There is nothing less inspiring than driving through a deserted campus unless it is viewing an empty chapel and locked community center. The most interesting part of seeing the church at work is the people who make all systems go. They can tell you how the mission came to be and what it hopes to become. The buildings only tell you what is here now and not even why.

Field trips are go and see tours, too, even in your own locality. Several steps preceding and following make the trip worth more than a day's diversion. In the first place, decide precisely what you want the group to see, and don't plan too much. Adults as well as children get tired and can't learn what is there to be grasped. Give the group some orientation: What are they to look for? Whom will they meet? Why are the people working there? Try to introduce a new experience characteristic of the area visited. A meal with chopsticks in Chinatown, a hoagie picnic in Philadelphia, a trip to the top of a fire tower on an Indian reservation, or a visit to the student-run farm at a resident school are all examples of everyday occurrences to some of the residents that can be memorable events to visitors.

Take few enough people or enough informed leaders

110

so that the tourists are able to ask questions and to hear well. Follow-up activities sometimes include writing for more information, inviting people from where you were to where you live, or further reading on that form of mission elsewhere. With a few people on the trip, individuals are more likely to want to continue a relationship.

Come and see trips put you on the receiving end. People are coming to see you, either on a return visit or because you represent the church at work in a new or unfamiliar way. No one can generalize about what visitors expect to see, but surely the best thing you can offer is the assurance that the mission of the church is carried on by human beings convinced that Christ's life makes the church's existence worthwhile. An inner-city mission project in an upper Middle West city involves a variety of good works and volunteers throughout the area. They have a steady stream of interested visitors. The head of the project says wryly: "We welcome everyone. We smile at the old who are hard of hearing; we tell the middle-aged how much it costs; we invite the young people to help us; and we make sure that the children want to come back and see us again."

Visitors can get in the way especially when they're unexpected. Try to remember, though, that without them you'd have a lot more rock to hoe in your own garden.

Go and help takes a tremendous amount of planning at both points. Young people and families sometimes volunteer a week in the summer in service to some mission of the church. It's sort of a domestic, short-term Peace Corps. Many times the cultural differences are vast, and it takes a great deal of getting used to by both hosts and visiting helpers. Most often the resident leader is the mediator and interpreter. Occasionally, he is a misfit in his job and his interpretation is a disservice to both those who come and those who live there.

When those who come camp out or have trailers, the living arrangements are fairly simple. Where the visitors are to live with the residents problems may arise. Getting up time in one western Pennsylvania community was 6:15 A.M. A college girl who had previously thought 7:30 A.M. the most uncivilized hour of the day, asked the unemployed man of the house, "Why do you get up so early when you've nothing to do?"

"Don't need anything to do, miss. It's the only time you can see the sun come over that hill there," the man answered. Her reasons for getting up in the morning had nothing to do with the natural world; they revolved around the demands of others. His were close to what was around him and less concerned with who was there and what they wanted of him.

With orientation beforehand, most people are eager to help and fare pretty well. It is wise to take a go and see tour before you decide to go and help. That is orientation in itself. Talking with those who have been to the place before can help a great deal, too, in making your trip useful to those you visit and enriching to you.

An affluent family from Connecticut became acquainted and then fond of a family and congregation in the Cumberland Mountains. The suburban woman became the envy of her neighborhood when her handwoven draperies and a colorful hooked rug were discovered. The woman explained that while Cal and her dentist-husband were out fixing teeth, she and her friend Mae had done a little "fancywork." What had started as a go and see side trip one summer continued as a go and help tour of duty and now is an annual visit with neighbors.

Family projects during the summer range from the trips we've been discussing to taking care of a child who needs a temporary home. Not all communities do this kind of foster home project, but where they do, there is sometimes no better place for a child. He knows he's visiting; he knows he will leave. In no other way should he be treated as temporary. A suburban family took a "difficult" twelve-year-old boy one summer. He arrived with his cardboard suitcase—empty. He was one of the family— a freewheeling foursome already. They proved to be shockproof and disarmingly frank.

"Mother!" John shouted, "E.G. has no pajamas."

"Well, give him a pair of yours," she shouted back. So it began. E.G. had no shorts and shirt, no bathing trunks, no toothbrush. E.G. didn't know how to eat scrambled eggs, had never had a tossed salad, and thought that a gallon carton of milk was the most milk there was in the world. For the first time in his life, E.G. was the most newsworthy, most fascinating story in the neighborhood. He was a star. He won everything at the swimming meet, he lost only to Peggy, his ten-year-old hostess, on the mile run, and came in last at tennis, a new game for him. The park program was like one long day at the circus for him; he never ran out of things to do or energy to try them.

At the end of the summer, he left with a few things in his suitcase to wear, a few blue and red ribbons to show, and the memory of a summer when he felt like a star. This was not the suburbanizing of E.G., as it might have been in another kind of family. It was his coming out party.

Families can do many things because they are Christians. The fact that it is summer gives them time in which to do them and often a place other than home. Thinking beyond yourself is a habit any time of the year. The church offers ideas to families who haven't thought of them and collects accounts of the rewards of service from those who have enjoyed working in the mission of the church. Don't waste your thinking and planning energy on ideas that have ceased to work when there are so many exciting variations you've never explored before.

WHAT ELSE DO WE DO IN THE YEAR?

A young minister came to a small church just outside a small village. He and his wife had decided to live somewhere away from the city and big-city churches. Both were suburban people, accustomed to using the resources of the city whenever they needed them. There was no library in the village, no drugstore, no doctor, no bakery—not much of anything but a bank, grocery store, and post office. The pulpit committee, pleased to find so able and young a man, asked about how the couple would get along in a place so different from their homes. "We're not like a lot of people," the chairman said. "Neither are we," the young man answered. "We'll take some getting used to."

The people in the church saw almost immediately what was meant. "He turns everything we've done inside out," clucked the postmaster. "The young people used to preach to us on Youth Sunday. Now this year they served us."

What the man has done consistently is to expect every baptized member over five years old to be a willing servant. Here are two examples.

Youth Sunday was observed by young people singing songs of the countries from where shut-ins', first, and then older people's ancestors came from. This involved research, which was collected all during the fall of the year in a program of visitation in which the young people took part. (They planned to get double mileage on their visits by planning the year in advance.) They practiced the songs, and then on Youth Sunday in February, took them from house to house.

"Oh Where and Oh Where Has Your Highland Laddie Gone?" "Du, Du Liegst Mir im Herzen," "Gray Birds Are Flying," and "MacNamara's Band" were the first four from Scotland, Germany, Iceland, and Ireland. At the Irish household the man taught them a *real* folk song, played his old fiddle rather badly, and taught them to do the Irish lilt.

The minister, never at a loss for an idea, and never too proud to admit his was not as good as someone else's, suggested the group of troubadours return to the other

114

houses and *receive* from them in return for the song. They heard folk tales, stories of the boat trip over, learned other songs, sang the doxology in Icelandic, and went on their way with an improvised and improved plan for the rest of their Youth Sunday of service to others.

Children's Day was a day to remember. There are no zoning rules to speak of in the open country, and in some parts of our country townships are careless about enforcing what laws they have. Next to the church was a vacant lot called "the junkyard" as opposed to a pit at the south end of the village called "the dump." One *took* things to the official dump, but things seemed to *land* in the unofficial junkyard. The worst or best of the suburbanite came out in the minister's wife every time she saw one more fender, old tire, or length of broken snow fence land in the vacant lot. So it was that the service of the children to the church on their day was to clean up the yard with the help of farmers in the congregation who owned half-ton trucks. Every child was there except one utterly disappointed second-grade boy with mumps, who had already missed his school picnic. They worked until three thirty on a hot Sunday in June. The grocer served them ice cream afterward on the cleared lot, and one of the directors of the bank gave each child a nickel and read the story Jesus told in Matthew, chapter 20, about each worker, no matter how long he worked, getting one silver coin. A sixth-grader remarked, "I see how those first guys felt when I consider my little brother got the same as I did for running around and being in the way."

The attitude of service was obviously catching on and was a welcome dimension to the church. Their calendar, aside from the ecclesiastical one, was made up completely of service. No one could possibly be confused by it.

It's time now for you to look back at your own year as an administrator in the church school, and to look at the possibilities for another year. Take some time to turn your hopes into goals. If you've always wanted good music and joyous singing in the church, don't just wish for it. Start *planning*. It can happen first in the church school. If you'd like to thank the teachers somehow, and wonder what to do, sit down and write a letter in longhand to each one. They don't need diplomas or gold seals. And if you have always admired the attractive room in the church across the street, call up a few friends, get some soap and water, and *clean*.

It's a worthy goal. It will offend no one, and you might even get a letter of appreciation from a teacher.

you are
the salt

Everyone remembers the best Sunday school teachers he has ever had. They are gifts from God. We don't have many good ones. If we all worked harder at supporting the souls who teach, the students would remember the better ones and have trouble thinking who among them was the best. That day may come. Hasten it by sound education.

You who support the teachers are the unsung heroes. Nobody thanks a coordinator, a superintendent, or an assistant in Christian education for teaching his child. You are not visible gifts. You may know every child by his name, and good coordinators do. The parents don't know this, and there is no specific reason they should find out. Much of what we do is done in a closet, and what is important is that good education comes, no matter who gets the credit. The stars in your crown come later, after the God who gives them decides whether or not a crown is in order.

You are the salt of the church school. And you must not lose your savor. You are the salt of the church. Tomorrow's church depends on today's for its leaders. The children in today's church are the leaders of tomorrow's.

It is enigmatic to work for no praise. We wonder if no one is watching us or if no one cares. We'll have to keep on working if we believe that service is gratitude for our space and place on earth. Nobody is paying for anything by working in the church. Jesus Christ paid for whatever we think we owe and more. Our service is extra. It is our way of saying thank you. Who cares if anyone sees us say thank you?

In a small town in New England a man who had been church school superintendent for many years died. The stand-in told the children, and one of the boys suggested that they all get excused from school for the funeral. The stand-in was dubious. "We'll sing his favorite hymns," the young leader pleaded. They did. "Lead On, O King Eternal" and "Our God, Our Help in Ages Past." What better legacy can a man pass on to the young?

There are those among us who say the church school should die and be resurrected in a form that is relevant to the demands of the day. Where the Scriptures are not taught, where boys and girls do not see men and women working in the name of Christ, and where no one cares that his faith is passed on and shared with others, there is no church school already. Where even one faithful man remains as teacher, a relevant church school exists. Relevancy is not merely novelty; it is the difference between living and dying. Those who know and tell the story of Jesus Christ by word and deed are relevant. Love of God and love of neighbor have stood the test of time. They do

118

not go in and out of style with educational techniques and jargon. Love knows no age.

Patience and the strength patience demands may sometimes appear to slip away from you. Those are the times we become children among children and need the grace of God as much as they. It is also the time to remember that there are those around us, children and adults alike, who do not know that we come to our God while we are petty and small, and he accepts us.

> "I sought the Lord, and he answered me,
>   and delivered me from all my fears.
> Look to him, and be radiant;
>   so your faces shall never be ashamed."

You are the salt of the earth.

appendix
songs for
an appreciation dinner

CHAPTER 1. THE VETERANS ON YOUR TEAM

HEY, CHRISTIANS! HO, CHRISTIANS!

(Music: "Nelly Bly")

RECRUITER: Come and teach! Come and teach!
We have need of you.
For once you taught ten four-year-olds
At Fort Waterloo.

RECRUIT: How do you know? Who told you so?
I'm new in church and town.
I'm Mrs. Anonymity.
You've turned me upside down.

RECRUITER: We wrote and told your minister
That you and Hank were here.
He answered: "Good! they both can teach.
Nab them when they appear."

RECRUIT: We will teach! We will teach
As we have done before.
But introduce us to your plant,
Your system, ways, and lore.

RECRUITER: We're just an ordinary church.
We teach and preach and pray,

And have Communion now and then.
What more is there to say?

RECRUIT: Where is our room? Where is the paste?
Where are the paints and clay?
Where are the teacher's guides and books?
Come, act before you pray!

ALL TEACHERS: Hey, Christians! Ho, Christians!
Listen while we say,
"We like to teach, but we beseech
You to act, then to pray."

CHAPTER 2. SCOUTING FOR AND TRAINING THE ROOKIES

I CAN DO IT!

(Music: "Oh! Susanna")

1.   Oh, I've taught the seventh-graders
Since my college boy was there.
I thought I couldn't do it,
But I took it on a dare.

Refrain:

I can do it!
I've done it and I know!
Visit any Sunday morning
And you'll find that it is so.

2.   The first day that I tried to teach
Erasers fell like rain.
The chalk and pencils joined them,
And I thought all was in vain.

Refrain

3.   The second day I'd had enough
Of seventh-grade horseplay.

122

I collected foreign objects
And kept school without delay.

Refrain

4. One day in deep midwinter
   Albert Gratz yelled, "Watch below!"
   Though I thought that he was joking,
   The whole room filled up with snow.

Refrain

5. We took them on an overnight,
   With tents, boots, eggs, and meat.
   We thanked our Lord for burned-up food,
   And came home with frozen feet.

Refrain

6. Oh, I like the seventh-graders,
   And they put up well with me.
   I intend to keep on teaching them
   Throughout posterity.

Refrain

CHAPTER 3. WHERE YOU'RE GOING AND WHY

COMMON SENSE

(Music: "Love's Old Sweet Song")

Once in the deep, dark winter of our souls,
We got together to think about our goals.
Teachers, administrators, pastor, too,
All asked the others, "What is it we do?"
When we convened, we were not playing games.
We looked at targets with well-thought-out aims.

Refrain:

So we formed objectives
For our church school year.

We know where we're going.
We're not idle here.
It is education
That we all dispense.
We must be good teachers;
That is common sense.
That is common sense.

CHAPTER 4. CLEANING THE HOUSE FOR ACTION

I'M NEW THIS YEAR

(Music: "Oh dem Golden Slippers")

Oh, I'm superintendent
And I'm new this year.
I came from Chattanooga
And was lonesome here.
But I joined the Presbyterians,
And was asked last spring
If I wouldn't give the Sunday school a fling.
Well, I visited in classes,
And I read each teacher's guide.
There will have to be improvements—
That I will confide.
But the problems all are soluble.
I know they're in our range,
If you Christians make your minds up, you can change.

Refrain:

Oh, we'll meet the problems,
But we'll beat the problems.
No one here would shed a tear
If they would disappear. (Hallelujah!)
We're behind the teachers,
And we're kind to teachers.
We want you here for this whole year.
You all come back, y' heah?

124

THE NON-CRISIS SONG

(Music: "The Flowers That Bloom in the Spring")

1. Things happen each week at the church,
> Tra la,

    But they are not crises as such.
    If there's paint on a sweater, so what?
> Tra la,

    We don't get excited that much,
> Tra la,

    We've developed what we call "soft touch."
    We've developed what we call "soft touch."
    And so we don't mean that we don't give a hoot
    If Bobby and Sally each have one wrong boot.
    Tra la la la la,
    Tra la la la la,
    We'll work it out to suit.

2. These things are non-crises; that's all,
> Tra la,

    Don't panic! Your life is too short.
    If you want to ask questions, just call,
> Tra la,

    We really intend to support,
> Tra la,

    Our calm attitude shouldn't appall.
    Our calm attitude shouldn't appall.
    You see, for real crises we're there to a man.
    We'll help you; we'll do everything that we can.
    Tra la la la la,
    Tra la la la la,
    Tra la la la la la!

CHAPTER 6. THE CHRISTIAN YEAR AND YOUR YEAR

AN ESTABLISHED PRO

(Music: "Silver Threads Among the Gold")

1. (Before)

LOUISE: Henry, it is Sunday morning.
It is funny-paper day.
Church school starts in half an hour—
Eat your eggs. Be on your way.

HENRY: But Louise, I told them I would quit
And make room for someone new.

LOUISE: Well, I told the pastor you'd serve
And coordinate the crew.

HENRY: Darling, I am growing, growing old.
I'm old-fashioned, I am told.

LOUISE: Don't you worry, Henry. I know
You are an established pro.

2. (After)

HENRY: Oh, Louise, I am encouraged.
Mrs. Hastings quit her post.
She gave me her resignation,
And said, "Henry, you're the most!"

LOUISE: Well, she never was a teacher, dear.
She made that profoundly clear.

HENRY: I knew that and figured she might.
What a joy to know I'm right!

LOUISE: Darling, you are growing, growing old.
You're old-fashioned, I am told.

BOTH: Let's not worry, for we both know
Who's a sharp, established pro!

CHAPTER 7. YOU ARE THE SALT

SONG FOR SUPERINTENDENTS

(Music: "Beautiful Dreamer")

Superintendents, this is your song!
If we've neglected you, we have been wrong.

Appreciation for all you've done!
And you've done everything under the sun.
Quieted babies, taught junior highs,
Kept our morale high without telling lies.
You are the faithful saints in disguise,
Salt of the earth folks who've opened our eyes!
Salt of the earth folks who've opened our eyes!

COMMITTEES COME, COMMITTEES GO

(Music: "Sweet Genevieve")

Committees come, committees go.
Because God loves us, he has it so.
But education of our young
Belongs to one that's yet unsung.
It gets the teachers every year.
It does not falter, faint, or fear.
It tries to see that all of us
Get our work done without a fuss.

Refrain:

Committees come, committees go,
And we in church would have it so.
With one exception to the rule—
The one that runs the Sunday school.

PASTORAL SYMPHONY

(Music: "Long, Long Ago")

1.
PASTOR: I am your pastor and you are my sheep.

SHEEP: Yes, we all know,
          That is quite so.

PASTOR: If you weren't helping, the hill would be steep.

SHEEP: Yes, we all know,
          Together we grow.

PASTOR: I want to thank you, and words won't suffice.
You are the pearls beyond world's price.

SHEEP: Don't mix your metaphors. Do be concise.
We already know
It is so.

2.
SHEEP: You stand behind us—lambs trembling with shock.

PASTOR: I try, but, lo,
I may be slow.

SHEEP: You don't desert us, the sheep of your flock.

PASTOR: I hope that's so,
As years come and go.

SHEEP: We don't expect you to praise and exhort.
All that we ask is your help and support.

PASTOR: I'll give you that. Don't you know I'm that sort?
I told you so,
And you know.

128